ANCIENT CHINESE WISDOM TO TRANSFORM YOUR BUSINESS: LESSONS FROM ZHENG HE, CONFUCIUS AND SUN ZI

DR MICHAEL TENG

Published in 2014 by Corporate Turnaround Centre Pte Ltd

Printed in Singapore by

All rights reserved.

ISBN-13:9789810913311

Printed ISBN: 978-981-09-1331-1

DEDICATION

This book is dedicated to my family members. They have given me all the encouragement, support and   assistance to write this book. It has taken more than three years to put together this book. But the teachings of the ancient wise people are ever green and this book is as relevant as the wisdom of our Chinese forefathers.

TABLE OF CONTENTS

ACKNOWLEDGMENTS

I would like to take this opportunity to acknowledge many people who have helped me to put together this book. I had to read some of the literatures and research materials in Mandarin as is relatively difficult to find materials written in English on this subject. Also, the Mandarin scripts are written in the ancient Mandarin style and thus I have to seek the Mandarin professionals who are familiar with such ancient Mandarin scripts for their interpretation. My heartfelt thanks also go to many who have helped me proof read the manuscript.

This book has taken me three years to write. I have many others to thank for making this journey a pleasant one, definitely less risky than the one undertaken by Admiral Zheng He six hundred years ago.

1. **WILL THE ASIANS RISE TO MEET THE CHALLENGE?**

Business leaders today, faced with stiff global competition and challenging external factors, must take a step back and learn to navigate seemingly insurmountable obstacles the smart way; the old way. As modern consultants and gurus vie to sell their wares: the latest and best practices which have sprung up over recent decades, corporate leaders must decide whether, in their need to rebuild, maintain, or improve profitability in the midst of these tumultuous external factors, they should simply take on board the expertise and advice offered by these consultants. Or, with the proof of corporate wisdom lying undoubtedly in the balance sheet, ongoing stock valuations and longevity of the enterprise, they need to start listening to their gut, which is telling them to dig deeper and start assessing the full scope of the problems: while they still have time.

It has been argued that the phenomenal success of the East Asian economies, when those in America and Europe have floundered, can be attributed to the fact that while the emphasis within Western economies has always been on free trade, civil liberties and shorter term goals, authoritarian regimes have seized the moment. With the likes of Taiwan, Korea, Singapore and Hong Kong, otherwise known as the economic tigers, rolling out aggressive government policies combined with a blanket adoption of free trade.

The situation is, of course, more nuanced than that. Taiwan and South Korea have become world leaders in information technology. Hong Kong and Singapore are widely regarded as international financial centers; with all four countries having an impressive ability to overcome major obstacles to growth and the spectacular bounce back by South Korea, following the crash from the Asian financial crisis is just one example of that resilience. For its part, China has also taken massive strides forward by opening up to the world economy and world trade organization, and as such is now prospering economically.

Could it be possible that there is a much simpler and more interesting explanation, for the success of the Asian economic tigers, over their Western counterparts? That it is the old fashioned Chinese values of hard work, transparency and thrift as espoused by ancient philosophers such as Zheng He, Confucius, and Sun Zi and which are still practiced by traditionalist Chinese citizens, and in the case of the teachings of Sun Zi, by Japanese businesses, that is responsible for such staggering financial success?

Western economies face numerous challenges. Self-stymied political leadership within the United States and the European Union, extremely competitive global labor markets, soft consumer demand, military expenses in a variety of theatres, tax revolts by the well-off, governance fiascos within major financial institutions, sovereign debt crises, and an aging population that will probably not be able to afford the required health care over the next decades. A greedy generation and unscrupulous entrepreneurs will never let corporate growth raise its head above them. It has to remain head and shoulder down. As such, it is my contention that modern Western corporations are in need of transformational leadership. Today's difficulties are significant and are deeply rooted in our cultural norms and expectations. We can best understand how to transform an enterprise by understanding the example of an exceptionally gifted leader, who was grounded in the philosophies of a highly successful culture.

We've been talking about problems in the world but no matter how much we talk about this, the problems do not seem to subside. Even as we talk; nothing ever changes. Indeed, more problems seem to arise, as more people discuss the issues. What is the reason behind this? There is a profound lack of models in which to approach these problems, and this has been a major cause: a difference in ideologies. Most of the challenges that the world is facing at the socioeconomic, political and environmental level arise from the ideological differences between the North and the South, as well as theoretical differences between Socialism and Communism versus Capitalism and Democracy, which are the best proponents of individualism and corporate greed.

The world is being ruled by Capitalism and Democracy, but they have failed us with Western cultural hegemony.

In fact, instead of solving our problems, Western imperialism has only aggravated, accentuated, and multiplied our problems. As such, we've become more enslaved than colonial slaves or slaves themselves. Considering this, then, we must search and find a new model other than what we are accustomed to. Which model will best serve our collective needs? Whichever we choose, it needs to recognize that we do not have universal solutions to particular problems and must try to address these problems with very different solutions. Will the model be from Africa? Asia? I would imagine that African hospitality would work well because, with African hospitality, Africa remains a jungle which is home to animals and humans alike; a jungle that is not controlled by enslaving rule, but by love which brings better order.

Asian wisdom is becoming prevalent with the revival of the philosophies of Asian personalities, such as, Mahatma Gandhi and Asian practices, such as, Taize. These have been tested at the personal level. At a more social level, there is typical Chinese wisdom tradition. First of all, the world's interest is turning toward China since it is gradually taking economic and political muscles over the United States and Europe. This is greatly boosted by BRICS, which is an economic body that has one advantage over the rest: numbers. As such, BRICS, will rule the world by the tyranny of numbers which will lower the cost of production and almost change demand into a kind of barter. We might not reach there anytime soon, but that is where we are heading towards. This will be a repudiation of the Malthussian principles and, probably, the Darwinian principle of survival of the fittest will be overturned, as well. Soon and very soon, we might start seeing the world move toward encouraging more births and discouraging abortion since we'll be trying to overcome Chinese numbers. Indeed, the world is cyclical and moves in a circle. This will be similar to the turn from "baby boomers" to a call for better order in the society and starting afresh to encourage morality, discipline, etc. However, the constitution of some countries, such as, the United States and many countries in Europe are facing a lot of resistances.

Chinese wisdom has been tested in China and also in many other parts of the world. Singapore is now banking on this, and she is developing by leaps and bounds. As such, we will further focus on ancient Chinese wisdom to see its applicability in different situations and, hopefully, critique and improve upon it. This has been done in many countries in Asia and now, the only remaining thing to do is test its universal value. This is the reason that I am embarking on writing this book.

The Confucian method of internal transformation has been effective in transforming governance and administration in China. This is mainly backed up by tough laws and decisive judiciary which adequately deal with cases of corruption, nepotism, discrimination, etc. As a result, China has significantly overcome the administrative weaknesses that other countries are facing. However, it is always important to rethink the independence of the judiciary as normative. Indeed, at the legislative and judicial level, China may have deviated from the means that were proposed by Confucius, especially, concerning steadfastness in administering justice and leniency. To some extent, Chinese law may have blocked the people from becoming aggressive enough in their business practices and, therefore, caused an economic backwardness in China itself.

China is, first of all, standing upon the size of her population and has to stamp her authority with this. She should become a model for other parts of the world, such as, Africa, India, and Latin America. There is a kind of paradox in these places because, despite their big population size, they continue to languish in poverty and domination. Indeed, instead of transforming the population size into market strength (demand – and - supply curves), they have been encouraged and persuaded that this is the beginning of their problems. In 1980, Ali A. Mazrui pointed out in his widely acclaimed book, The African Condition: A Political Diagnosis, a number of evils that these nations are facing.

China has not completed the metamorphosis. She still has a lot to do at the international (diplomatic) and economic level. China suffers from air-pollution, and corruption is rampant which President Xi is trying hard to address, credit and shadow banking problems and corporate governance and ethical problems with several of her major companies. It is apparent that Chinese (along with Korean) politics are often a secretive matter. To achieve this metamorphosis China will have to team up with the

Arab world (which has, to a greater extent, defied Western domination) and Africa. She has already stamped her authority in various parts of Asia, although religious ideology is still an obstacle in some of these parts – such as Philippines, Vietnam, etc.

China is leading the economic growth in the world. In China, we can find a large concentration of successful, growing companies that thrive, despite the problems in the environment. China is the world's current economic powerhouse. This is evident in the fact that China holds about 36% of America's foreign-held US Treasury securities and, according to CNN Money's Report for 2010, three of the top twenty-five fastest-growing companies in the world also have their headquarters in China. Except for Canada's top-ranked El Dorado Gold, with a head office in British Columbia, the rest are all located in the USA.

IN THIS CORNER, THE ODDS-ON FAVOURITE

How has China gained its competitive edge? What were the triggers which led to this success? In order to find these answers, I believe that we must look to China's ancient cultural wisdom and philosophers. China's population has defied all odds and theories including Malthusianism. There are real indications that China, which is already the second largest economy is gearing up to overtake the U.S.A as the world's largest economy. At the time of writing this book, the most recent report by the International Comparison Program (ICP) which

12

works alongside the World Bank places China's GDP at just under eighty seven percent of the U.S.A's GDP, compared to forty-three percent in 2005. Further, despite the fact that the world is moving towards democracy and capitalism, which is the twin sister of democracy, China's growth has been greatly boosted by Chinese socialist and totalitarian tendencies. Finally, there is the entrepreneurial spirit of China - China has been, for centuries, a primary producer and consumer of goods trading between the Mediterranean, Africa, and Middle East.

Although China's rise as an economic powerhouse is relatively recent, it should not be attributed to new philosophies or approaches because China is slowly retreating from its commitment to Maoist Communism while simultaneously reverting to its deeper philosophical foundations. A broad range of ancient Chinese wisdom and advice has stood the test of time guiding Chinese attitudes and practices for centuries. Today, China is reaping the benefits from this wisdom.

Certain Chinese philosophers represent a broad range of Chinese wisdom. Sun Zi's "The Art of War" and the philosophy of Confucius may be known by reputation but are not known in sufficient detail in the Western world. Lesser-known teachings include Lao Tzu's "Tao Te Ching." While divination may not be an acceptable practice in modern boardrooms, the "I Ching" is one foundation of Chinese culture and is relied upon by many philosophers and leaders. Tao Zhu Gong specifically dealt with retail marketing. His insights and practices remain a source of guidance in the modern setting.

In contrast to all of these philosophers, Admiral Zheng He was the foremost promoter of Chinese commercial interests using Chinese ancient wisdom in the 15th century. His expeditions are famous in the Orient but are not well known in the West. Yet, he did collaborate with a variety of foreign dignitaries as he pursued both diplomacy and trade. In Chapter 8, I will look in detail at how Admiral Zheng He is influencing the modern day corporate transformation process. So, not only will this book provide an overview of ancient Chinese wisdom and philosophies, it will also offer an in-depth review of Zheng's achievements and methods, It will also demonstrate how he used or modified the wisdom whose origins were derived from the teachings of earlier Chinese sages and is essential reading not only for business leaders seeking a transformational path, but also anyone seeking a more enlightened and fulfilling path in life.

2. CHINA IN THE GLOBAL CONTEXT OF ECONOMIC UPHEAVALS AND PROBLEMS

What would the differing global economies look like today, I wonder if the West were to embrace the ideologies of these ancient Chinese Philosophers? Like many European countries, the USA is heavily in debt, and while, at the time of writing this book, it is Barack Obama's Democrat Party that holds the presidency, time moves fluidly and the Republican Party is strongly committed to lower taxes, at least, for the wealthy. While the Democrats are widely regarded as being less hawkish, the Republicans are also focused on maintaining and utilizing the largest military force on the planet. In The Art of War, Sun Zi noted that it is expensive for a country to remain on a war footing. He also said that rulers would have trouble maintaining their popularity if the peasants were overly burdened by taxes.

Recent history has shown that any weakness in the US economy, whether perceived or real, ricochets and reverberates around the rest of the world. Junk bonds and toxic asset-based securities wreak havoc all the way from Wall Street to Fleet Street and beyond.

By the middle of 2011, the European sovereign debt crisis had started to overshadow American economic problems, would weakness in Greece or Portugal derail the mighty German powerhouse? Would national politics and sovereignty take a back seat to the need for liquidity in the European financial markets? This situation, whilst gradually improving, is still volatile in 2014.

The Middle East remains a quagmire for foreign intervention, however, well-intentioned or selfish it seems. Ethnic tensions within Israel-Palestine and perennial mistrust across its borders with Arab nations ensure that the long history of conflict will continue. Elections have now been held in most of the countries affected by the Arab Spring, and while the situation in many of those countries still rests on a knife edge, one can only hope, that some kind of order will prevail. Who can say though, whether emerging regimes that are not favored by Washington will be allowed to flourish, or whether they will be destabilized in the name of Western economic interests?

Terrorism or perhaps "nationalistic freedom fighting" continues within the nations of India and Pakistan, in a blend of disputes over territory, religious heritage, and the opportunity to control economic levers.

Finally, the disagreements over climate change seem to be based more on religious beliefs or economic dreams than on scientific observations. We humans find it difficult to focus on long-term threats when the required remedy involves immediate sacrifice. Has the threat of global warming been over-stated? Or are we resigned to the inevitable flooding of the many highly populated cities bordering the world's oceans because the problem is not, in fact, under human control at all?

REPEATED DROUGHT AND FAMINE

The drought in the Horn of Africa captured the world's attention, back in 2011. Historically, when Somalia and Kenya have missed out on their winter rains, crops have failed, and both livestock and people have suffered. However, the cause of this region's recurring droughts is recognized to be the La Niña oceanic current and whenever the Pacific's current off South America cools, even just by a few degrees, worldwide rainfall patterns shift. Without an alternative source of fresh water, north-eastern Africa will experience famine on a fairly recurring basis.

It is worth noting that the El Niño – La Niña temperature changes cause variations in weather patterns in many other parts of the world. Excess rainfall and drought shift depending on this one current, whose temperature will no doubt continue to fluctuate as it has for centuries. The question is whether people will find ways to pro-actively deal with the effects.

GREED VERSUS FINANCIAL REGULATIONS: PRODUCT SAFETY, WORKPLACE SAFETY, AND ENVIRONMENTAL REGULATIONS

Many articles have been written aimed solely at dissecting the greedy and misguided attempts to profit from junk bonds and arcane financial derivatives in the last decade. Some analysts have claimed that the regulators were fooled; others that the regulators were hamstrung by the very rules governing their attempts to safeguard the markets.

On an ongoing basis, financial regulators and corporate auditors must also ensure that companies comply with regulations that govern financial reporting and disclosure. A minority might have reported that human greed continues to motivate all but the most saintly philanthropists. It is human nature to seek advantage over competitors. Those who find opportunities to outsmart the regulations have much more to gain, both personally and for the companies they represent, than do the regulators.

From time to time, companies are found to have built unsafe products or sold contaminated foods or medicines. Regulations are in place to promote safe practices in the workplace. Yet, employees are injured due to lack of compliance with safety standards which include everything ranging from uninstalled safety equipment to fatigue due to long working long hours. This kind of working environment tends to be dangerous, and can cause physical illnesses, as well. In fact, in certain jobs, you may have work-related injuries, such as, loss of eye-sight and lung cancer. This is something that can be easily avoided with proper understanding and care.

While many countries have regulations to protect the environment, we still learn of sudden disasters such as oil spills and simmering conditions such as toxic mine tailings.

The costs of protecting the health and safety of

customers, workers, and the environment can be weighed against penalties for non-compliance and, perhaps, greater profits can be realized if a company retains a sterling reputation and keeps their workers and customers alive and well.

SHORT-TERM VERSUS LONG-TERM VIEWS

The financial markets usually report results quarterly. The twin comparisons are "this quarter over the last quarter" and "this quarter over the same quarter of last year." Few investors check how any given company has performed over a decade. At the rate of change in many industries, perhaps few companies could be compared to themselves over that time frame.

It is obvious that companies should take on a wider view, one that is focused on what may occur within their working months – and possibly, years down the line. At least, it is obvious when considering, for example, maintenance and refurbishment of capital assets such as factories. On second thought, this may not be too obvious if the run-down condition will be used as an excuse to outsource production to a low-cost offshore partner.

Politicians face a similar situation. The next campaign begins before the elected official has even been sworn into office. It is increasingly difficult to capture voters' attention for substantial issues, and nearly impossible to gain consent for a course of action with long-term benefits if there are short-term costs.

DEVELOPING PROBLEMS IN INDIA

India has been an economic tiger for several decades. It combines a well- educated urban labor force that has grit and determination, international connections at both the state and personal levels, and an agricultural backbone. It often ranks second to China in economic statistics such as annual GDP growth. Unfortunately, several of its problems may be moving from "simmer" to boil."

There are concerns for infrastructure, especially for transportation such as rail lines and trucking. Difficulties in shipping fresh farm produce to urban markets have been blamed for price inflation and food shortages. India's geography presents a challenge to transportation: the mountains and valleys do not ease the task of creating rail or road links across the country. As well, some say that either the government is intrinsically slow to respond or has corrupt officials who can delay projects until bribes are paid.

Are these problems real? Could they just be the perceptions of those who are eager to succeed, but have not yet been able to? Do these problems become more pressing as more citizens achieve a measure of economic success?

Also, India has a long-standing feud with Pakistan. It is difficult to predict whether, or not, this situation will improve in either the short or medium term.

DOES CHINA FACE SIMILAR ISSUES?

In late 2011, the government of China began to speak in favor of preserving the environment at the Durban summit. This runs counter to the usual opinion that China will pursue its own economic interests regardless of pollution or greenhouse gas emissions. Is this a sign that China's economy is "mature enough" to look beyond immediate growth? (At the same time, the USA and Canada are debating whether and where to place a new oil pipeline. Part of the tension pits immediate economic benefits against the potential contamination of a major American aquifer).

Environmental and property ownership concerns have also been raised for at least one hydro-electric project in China. Again, it may be a sign of political maturity that people might openly protest when their personal interests run counter to those of the state.

As noted earlier, one of the great challenges China faces is that its success may outstrip the ability of its trading partners to maintain the pace. Already there has been pressure to allow the currency to fluctuate as a way of making Chinese exports more expensive and thus to protect foreign manufacturers. Moreover, China has made significant investments in foreign territories, explained in part by the need to spend some of its foreign exchange surplus by purchasing assets.

In 2011, China had remarkable economic power. As American politicians debated raising its debt ceiling, with

Democrats and Republicans arguing about spending cuts versus tax cuts, China quietly reminded them that a huge portion of that debt is owed to China. During a recent round of tension between North Korea and South Korea, the world looked to China to act as a broker between these states.

China is a major importer of raw materials, making it extremely important to countries such as Canada that "hew wood and draw water." At the same time, China processes those raw materials and sells the finished goods at low prices. The balance of trade is extremely favorable to China.

China has retained a low valuation on its currency, helping to maintain that favorable balance of trade. Although it has been criticized for not allowing its currency to float, China has not been forced to do so. One wonders whether any other country or economic bloc would be capable of forcing China to take such action.

Also, as reported by CNN Money, China had three of the top 25 fastest-growing companies in the world for 2010, which are the companies of Sohu.com, Zhongpin, and China Automotive Systems. In 2013, it was still managing to punch above its weight globally, with Baidu featuring in the top 30.

SOHU.COM

Sohu.com was rated the 12th fastest growing company in the world in 2010. Sohu is an Internet company, and whose name when translated as "Search Fox," aptly describes its business. Google is, of course, the dominant search engine company in the world; it makes its name by quickly delivering useful and up-to-date search results. Their revenue also comes from selling advertising on the browsing pages as well as on web pages in partnership with web hosts. Its size and cash reserves allow Google to test many other revenue streams and possible markets.

Sohu also provides search engine capabilities, online advertising, and multi-player online games. It was awarded the contract to host the Beijing Olympic Games' online web site.

In 2011, Sohu won a lawsuit restricting Google from using a specific pinyin input editor, having claimed that Google infringed on Sohu's copyright.

ZHONGPIN

Zhongpin was listed as the 17th fastest growing company worldwide during 2010. It is a significant agribusiness player, with a focus on hog processing and marketing. They also have stakes in fruit and vegetables companies. Zhongpin's stock is listed and trades in the United States

Investment advisor "Seeking Alpha" reported in August 2011 that Zhongpin may have been engaged in "possible fraudulent activities" with respect to financial reporting and disclosure, and in November 2012 it was announced that Levi & Korsinsky were investigating possible breaches of fiduciary duty. This seems to demonstrate that sadly, not every Chinese company abides by the principles of honesty and integrity which served Zheng He and his contemporaries so well.

CHINA AUTOMOTIVE SYSTEMS

Ranked 23rd worldwide for growth in 2010, China Automotive Systems, manufacturer parts for cars. Its focus is on power steering systems and components, both for commercial and private automobiles. Although it has both domestic and foreign factories and alliances, its major market is the growing automotive manufacturing industry within China.

This company does face competition within China. Ford Motor Co., for example, has announced plans to invest in Jiangling Motors Co. and construct a new factory in China. Whether this venture would produce parts for export for Ford, or whether Ford plans to sell automobiles in China, is not yet clear. China Automotive Systems are listed on the NASDAQ stock exchange.

BAIDU

Baidu is an internet Chinese language search engine company and is widely regarded as the Chinese equivalent of Google. It was founded in 2000, by Robin Li, creator of Hyperlink Analysis (A form of search technology) and since then the company has enjoyed phenomenal growth. In addition to its core search engine product, Baidu is also behind several community based products, for example, Baidu Encyclopedia; the world's largest Chinese language encyclopedia.

Baidu launched its Institute of Deep Learning in 2013 and has made considerable progress in the fields of image and voice recognition as well as semantic intelligence. It now has its sights firmly set on the field of Artificial Intelligence, announcing on May 16[th,] 2014, the appointment of a widely respected Artificial Intelligence researcher, Andrew Ng. Ng will now head up Baidu Research, with laboratories both in China and the Silicon Valley, in the U.S.A. This emphasis on Artificial Intelligence is an incredibly exciting step forward, as Baidu races against other technological giants to bring the very latest in cutting edge technology to us.

All of these companies are an example of Chinese strength and agility in rising to the top, and Sun Zi would be proud of the accomplishments, if not in the case of Zhongpin, the methods applied. Baidu and its contemporaries have found out their competition's strengths and weaknesses and have risen above them by not only presenting a more improved product, but by actively head-hunting the most talented individuals on the planet, and investing heavily in research and future growth.

3. HOW CULTURAL PHILOSOPHY SHAPES NATIONAL AND CORPORATE DECISION

There is a classic question that asks, "Which came first, the chicken or the egg"? In the realm of politics, a similar question that can be addressed is, "Which is the cause and which the effect: cultural philosophy versus national decisions"?

Political actions can neither arise nor be sustained unless the culture is at least primed to follow. If a country's leaders successfully pursue a policy of military aggression for several generations, then the surviving citizens will undoubtedly live in a culture that sets high value on warfare. If the leaders instead choose to cultivate trade and commerce, then the culture will espouse negotiation and wealth. By contrast, if the rulers set a course too radical for their followers to appreciate, then they will not receive the necessary support from the population.

For example, in the nineteenth century, the general population of the U.S.A was broadly of the opinion that it was the destiny of American settlers to expand throughout the whole of the continent, and in what became known as the Manifest Destiny Doctrine. History saw ordinary citizens willingly taking up arms to enter into armed conflict with Britain in 1812, as they clashed violently at Lake Erie over the fate of Canada, before turning their attention to Texas and California; locking horns with Mexico as part of the process of laying down the borders of the contiguous 48 states.

By contrast, the United States was wallowing in a period of isolationism prior to each of the World Wars. World War I began in Europe during the summer of 1914, but the policy of non-intervention kept the USA out of this war until April 6, 1917. World War II began on September 1, 1939 with the invasion of Poland, but the USA remained "officially neutral" whilst covertly providing material aid to the Allies, until the attack on Pearl Harbor on December 7, 1941.

With its large size and history of developing wilderness into towns and cities, the United States has extensive suburban housing and has worked on the assumption that more farmland will always be available. Towns in rural France or Japan, in contrast, are often tightly contained within historical boundaries to ensure the continued agricultural use of land.

The American sense of independence and self-reliance is reflected by the relative ease of an individual to start a small business in the United States in contrast to more onerous restrictions found in Europe, while Switzerland provides us with another perfect example of cultural philosophy in motion. She has remained stoical in her decision to forego alliances and remain neutral militarily since 1815. A big part of this decision seems to have stemmed from her annexing by France in 1798, when Switzerland became essentially a satellite state under French control. Within a few years, the people living in Switzerland refused to fight for France against the

Russian and Austrian invaders and by 1815, Switzerland was recognized as independent and neutral. This violation of her territory seems to have become deeply embedded within her psyche, as, over the next 35 years, a constitution was developed which included Article 11, forbidding sending troops abroad: a law which the country still upholds to this date. Is it a coincidence, or has the fact that Switzerland has not wasted her resources, or citizen's lives on waging war, the reason for her staggering wealth? A report by leading financial institution, Credit Suisse, has cited Switzerland as having the highest nominal wealth per adult in the world. Is this a lesson that leaders around the globe could learn from, I wonder?

North Korea has a long history isolationism but paradoxically has long-standing conflicts with South Korea as well as some positive ties with Russia and China. To what extent does this reflect an innate cultural tendency? How much should be attributed to the founding and "Eternal President" Kim II Sung's personal preferences? Kim II -Sung wrote and promoted the concept of "Juche"6, incorporating economic self-reliance and independence from other powerful nations. Perhaps more importantly, given that vast swathes of the world appear to be on a war footing, and North Korea, under the leadership of Kim Jong Un, is definitely on Western radars at the moment, how will cultural philosophy sway the country's military decisions in the immediate and long term future?

In the Middle East, many countries with a strong respect

for a patriarchal social structure have been traditionally slow to move toward democracy, or so it may seem to a modern European or American steeped in traditions of youthful rebellion, (for example, the French Revolution; Britain's Magna Carta; the American Revolution). While many Westerners struggle to comprehend both the cultural and political systems that are deeply ingrained within this part of the world, it is a fact that Middle Eastern countries have a long history of maintaining close ties between cultural and religious influences. Both the culture and religion respect the role of the eldest male to lead his family, and villages look to the "elders" for leadership. Is it right that people from nations, whose society is stacked in favor of the young and healthy, often at the expense of their more experienced elders, should criticize and condemn nations over which frankly, they have no knowledge: just because their cultural belief systems are not in alignment with their own?

Most of the Middle Eastern countries have thousands of years of history. Israel, of course, looks back to Biblical times and the strength of the kingdom ruled by David and his son Solomon. Their view of the right to govern Israel-Palestine derives, at least in part, from Judaism. The 20th Century Holocaust may also transform their view that Jewish people are not truly safe in other countries or even in their homeland unless they have the means to defend it.

During the Libyan uprising in 2011, Muammar Gaddafi often called the Western nations "crusaders." While the term is usually one of approval in Western cultures, people of Islamic heritage will think of the western people in a similar way to the invaders from Europe. (The First Crusade was launched by Pope Urban II in 1095 AD. The Ninth Crusade was in 1271-2 and lesser, but equally divisive crusades were waged as late as the 15th Century.) Gaddafi's death was seen as a moment of victory for the uprising. Has Libya become a better, safer place to live since the removal of Gadaffi and is the democratically elected government, delivering on its promises to the people? Unfortunately, it would appear not. Prime Minister Ali Zeidan was forced to flee the country in May 2014 after the parliament voted him out of office. Militia groups are rife, and the country is in disarray. Was it really worth the billions of dollars that it collectively cost the coalition partners to remove Gadaffi? Is it time that the U.S.A and its European partners maybe started looking to the teachings of ancient philosophers such as Zheng He and Sun Si? And rather than being so quick to judge and rush to war, perhaps, consider a more conciliatory path?

It has often been said that Afghanistan has a history of being unconquerable. The Soviet Union tried by military means and failed to gain influence there. After some 14 years battling the Taliban and with 3,435 coalition deaths (This figure is accurate as of 30th April 2014), it seems unlikely that Western democracies will achieve or maintain their full goals after the planned troop withdrawals towards the end of 2014, meanwhile, the country which is steeped in ancient traditions and ways will simply carry on as it always has: no matter how morally repugnant, Western nations find the concept. Are there lessons to be learned from this, I wonder? Will even those cultural philosophies that have been born of violence, yet which have been embedded within a nation's psyche for millennia, always prevail over outside influence? What would Admiral Zheng He say?

THREE MAJOR PHILOSOPHIES THAT SHAPED CHINA

In contrast to the cultural philosophies of other countries, China has demonstrated three major behavioral patterns over the centuries. Each pattern either reflects one of three philosophies or is drawn from a blend of those philosophies.

COLLABORATION: ADMIRAL ZHENG HE

Admiral Zheng He may possibly be the most famous Chinese ambassador, admiral, diplomat, and trade emissary of all time. China's current and past leaders consider Zheng He, whose name is sometimes spelled "Cheng Ho," a pivotal example and have lined up to praise him highly. Hu Jintao, who was President of China, until 2012 said, "In the 15th century, the Ming Dynasty sent Zheng He to Australia, and he contributed greatly to the economy of Australia." While Wen Jiabao, also the Prime Minister of China until 2012 said, "Zheng He, was a great diplomat. All of his voyages were to bring friendship, wealth, gifts, and technology to benefit the countries that he visited. The Chinese are indeed kind and magnanimous." Meanwhile, Jiang Zemin, the President from 1993 to 2003 has said,

"Zheng He's voyages were very impressive. They showed that the Chinese people were trying to make friends with their neighbors and interact with them for mutual economic and cultural benefits. These resulted in the rapid progress of the world."

Even the father of modern-day China, Deng Xiaoping, Paramount Leader of the Communist Party said, "Zheng He, demonstrated that China needs to be open. The Ming Dynasty was one of the more prosperous eras in Chinese history because of Zheng He, opening up China to the world."

He's story began in 1403 A.D., which was when Zhu Di usurped the imperial throne of China in 1403 to become Emperor Yong Le. Yong Le continued to follow the foreign policies of his predecessor, Emperor Taizu. These policies could be summarized as follows: defend Chinese borders against incursion; maintain peaceful and friendly relations with neighboring countries, and encourage foreign trade, including the receipt of tribute from allied nations.

China's most important international commerce included at that time, selling tea, spices, silk, and ceramics. Trade routes included overland caravans and the sea. Since ceramics was heavier than spices, these goods were better suited to transportation by ship.

Emperor Yong Le made one change, which was to promote trade by means of pro-active diplomacy. His probable motive was to establish himself as the internationally recognized emperor of China, but he also realized that the method would have the benefit of strengthening both diplomatic and trade relationships with a large number of other countries: tasks which he assigned to Zheng He.

Admiral Zheng He made seven grand voyages in total; the first six of which were for Emperor Yong Le. Zheng He's legacy was that of collaboration: he actively sought to win the cooperation of foreign rulers, when he could have instead attempted to be heavy-handed and domineering.

CONFRONTATION: SUN ZI AND THE ART OF WAR

His name is sometimes spelled "Sun Tzu," "Sun Zi" or "Sun Wu." Sun Zi lived sometime during the Spring and Autumn period of China, which was 722-481 BCE, and probably towards the end of that period. The Spring and Autumn period was a time of transformation in China: a time when the power of the ancient Zhou Kings faded, and fiefdoms gained their independence. Sun Zi wrote his infamous book, The Art of War, during this period, and the book was to prove to be incredibly influential during the next epoch of Chinese history; otherwise known as the Warring States period.

Fighting amongst themselves, the Chinese states used military force to consolidate or extend their territories.

The period of the Warring States (479-221 BCE) saw a change from feudal and chivalric warfare to professional generals who ruthlessly sought every advantage in tactics and deployment.

This was then followed by the beginning of the Imperial Era. The Emperors began the Great Wall as a means of defending the unified country from Northern raiders. To over-simplify, one thousand years of history China went through break-ups and reunifications   much of its military effort was expended internally, and most of the rest of their military strength was aimed at preventing foreign invasions.

The Art of War has been studied throughout China by military leaders while politicians and business leaders have found inspiration and guidance from its precepts. It has also been translated into many languages. One translator, Samuel B. Griffith, claimed that Sun Zi's book influenced Mao Tse-Tung.

CO-EXISTENCE: CONFUCIUS

Tradition says that Confucius lived from 551-479 BCE, which would have made him a contemporary of Sun Zi. Despite having been born in a family of the "noble warrior" class, Confucius grew up in poverty before becoming a justice minister in his home province. Confucius later resigned that position and spent a number of years travelling and teaching.

Confucian philosophy pursues self-improvement as demonstrated and exercised in relating properly with others. Confucianism is a predominant philosophy in China, Japan, Korea, Taiwan, and Vietnam. Even in modern Communist China, Confucianism continues to play a role, for example, Chiang Kai-shek's New Life Movement used Confucianism, among other ideas, to counter Soviet Communist ideology and to create a more idealistic and healthier Chinese culture.

OTHER CHINESE PHILOSOPHERS

Many other philosophers have made an impression on Chinese thought and culture. However, compelling these individuals were, this book will only touch on a few.

Lao Tzu is credited with introducing Daoism by writing the Tao Te Ching. This potent combination of religion and philosophy has strongly influenced Chinese thought.

Tao Zhu Gong wrote advice for merchants and business owners in the form of brief aphorisms and pearls of wisdom. Those wishing to understand Chinese mercantilism should start with Tao Zhu Gong's writings.

The I Ching, or what is better known as the "Book of Changes," is attributed to an almost mythical personage as well as credited to later historical figures. The I Ching can be seen as a tool for divination, but it embodies a philosophy that values opposites that complement each other. The phrase "yin and yang" is, but one way that the I Ching has influenced the Western thought.

Zhuge Liang, a military strategist like Sun Zi, who

became famous during the time when China had three kingdoms. His strategies had reduced many casualties during the battles. However, they are not as widely used in corporations as Sun Zi's strategies.

A PRAGMATIC APPROACH TO PHILOSOPHY

A nation will make its decisions, whether through politics or as individuals, based on its beliefs, underlying assumptions, and philosophies. As circumstances change and opportunities arise, the country's philosophical outlook will determine its response.

While academics and dreamers may debate that, along the theoretical merits of any world view, business leaders should use history and economics to review the results of these philosophies. In a real and pragmatic sense, the countries that thrive demonstrate that they have integrated the most potent and useful philosophies as the foundations for their success.

It is not just global and business leaders that can benefit from looking backwards in order to move forwards in life. We live in an incredibly stressful, consumerism world, where the pressure to own the biggest house in the best neighborhood, drive the flashiest car, and send our children to the most exclusive schools can at times be overwhelming. When the pressure on us both mentally and physically to prove to our peers as well as the wider community that we are somehow super-human, the stress is immense. Yet we find ourselves lacking the time and resources to complete even the most basic of tasks.

It is time like this that we need to take stock of our lives and seriously question the path that we have chosen to follow. Your geographical location; the place where you are born, as well as the people who nurture and feed you, will clearly have a significant impact upon your world view, for example, a girl growing up in Afghanistan is going to have different expectations and prospects due to her cultural heritage, than a girl growing up in Washington, or New York. Likewise, a boy growing up under the watchful eye of his high-flying father in Hong Kong or Tokyo is going to have different life experiences and therefore a higher chance of succeeding than his peer growing up in the wrong part of Chicago, or Detroit.

What most of us have yet to grasp is that it's not where we come from that matters, it's our final destination that counts.

Drawing upon both Eastern and Western Spiritual and Metaphysical traditions, the New Age Movement, which harnesses elements of many world religions, including Buddhism, Taoism, Christianity, Sufism and even Chinese Folk Religion, began to capture the hearts and imaginations of many Westerners in the late twentieth century, who were both disenchanted with their lives and disillusioned with the hollow words coming out of the establishment and who were therefore desperately searching for a deeper purpose: direction in their directionless lives. So while many people were happy to embrace the writings of the likes of Emanuel Swedenborg, and started to look to astronomy and alchemy for answers, or cherry-picked the elements of various different religions that suited, while disregarding other aspects, then the philosophies of the likes of Zheng He, Sun Zi, Confucius and other ancient Chinese philosophies with 5000 years of history, which are absolutely brimming with solutions to everyday business problems, were sadly overlooked.

4. CONFLICT: SUN ZI AND "THE ART OF WAR"

Although there is no hard evidence to corroborate this, it is generally accepted that Sun Zi died sometime after 500 BCE. He had served King Helü of the Wu state as a military general from about 512 BCE, and as already discussed in the previous chapter, Sun Zi's "The Art of War" has been influential in military training and other competitive endeavors ever since it was written.

SUN ZI'S MAJOR WORK: THE ART OF WAR

Sun Zi provides a compelling overview by outlining five "constant factors" to consider when planning a campaign.

1. **The Moral Law** - Anybody who is a king must be well-trained and regarded as morally fit to command the army because he will be risking human lives in battle.
2. **Heaven** - Warfare depends on the environment. The general who ignores the changing environment is doomed.
3. **Earth** - Warfare also depends on the terrestrial environment: the distance to be covered; the terrain; ground cover or natural ambush locations.
4. **The Commander** - The leader must be wise, sincere, kind or humane, brave and strict.
5. **Methods and Discipline** - The army must march in order, under officers of varying ranks. It must also maintain supply lines and control its costs. So a general must determine which army is favored in these categories.

Sun Zi also elaborated upon the importance of deception to fool the enemy about strengths, deployment, movements, timing and goals.

THE CHAPTERS OF "THE ART OF WAR"

Anyone wishing to gain a deeper insight into what Sun Zi was saying should analyze the book thoroughly. There have been many translations of The Art of War. The version under discussion now uses R.D. Sawyer's chapter titles.

WAGING WAR

A prolonged campaign wears out one's own army. Sun Zi solves supply problems by foraging on enemy soil, rather than carrying excess provisions or - horrors! - returning home for supplies. Sun Zi notes that the government cannot afford lengthy campaigns. He also advises rewarding soldiers, particularly those who led the charges and captured the plunderer.

PLANNING OFFENSIVES

This chapter is also titled "Attack by Stratagem" and recommends capturing countries, armies, or squads rather than destroying them. Following from the previous chapter's desire for speed, Sun Zi advises against siege warfare: it simply takes too long to set up, or the attacker will lose patience, attack prematurely, and be defeated.

An army with overwhelming advantages can win without killing. Rulers cannot govern an army using civilian methods; nor should generals command a country using military discipline.

THE FIVE ESSENTIALS FOR THE VICTOR ARE:

1.   Knowing when to fight or not;
2.   Knowing how to handle superior odds or inferior odds;
3.   Having high morale and shared goals throughout the army;
4.   Being prepared and attacking when the enemy is unprepared; and
5.   Having military capacity without interference from the civilian ruler.

MILITARY DISPOSITION

First, deploy forces defensibly, to avoid the possibility of defeat.   Second, when the opportunity arises, attack swiftly and without reservation when the enemy is vulnerable.

Truly skillful generals will not receive a lot of praise because the victories will seem easy. Planning is important: Sun Zi again refers to "Earth" for calculating distances and thus, the odds of success.

STRATEGIC MILITARY POWER

Commanding an army is like commanding a few soldiers: it requires a leadership pyramid to pass down the orders to manageable numbers of followers.

A few ingredients can give rise to many flavors, so a combination of direct and indirect tactics can provide endless combinations for victory. The idea is to keep the enemy busy on one front, but also attack the flanks and the rear.

Lengthy preparations may be necessary before a sudden and decisive attack. In order to deceive the enemy by feigning weakness or disorder, one's army must be extremely well-disciplined, because by doing so, it may be possible to elicit enemy movement, such as to have them attack into an ambush.

Use the right people, but do not rely on any one individual's heroic efforts. He teaches that an army must function as a unit, and ensure that the whole troop advances together, swiftly, at the right time.

VACUITY AND SUBSTANCE

The chapter, which is also known as "Weak and strong" places emphasis on being at the right place and time: to your advantage and to your opponent's disadvantage. Attack when and where the enemy is unprepared or weak; defend impregnable fortresses.

If the enemies do not know your deployment, they must guard everywhere; you can then concentrate an attack on one fraction of the enemy's forces. You might also prevent their attack by deceiving them as to your strengths.

The chapter returns to distance and time concerns: only through careful planning can several wings of an army meet for a decisive battle, after starting in different places. Poor planning prevents one group from supporting another.

Military strategy is subtle and difficult for most to understand, even if a particular strategy seems obvious in hindsight. A wise general changes tactics from battle to battle, even if the principle remains the same. Just as seasons alternate, so too must a general's tactics.

MILITARY COMBAT

Organize the army and mislead the enemy about destination and capabilities, and then move quickly to secure the preferred battleground before the enemy can. However, the haste cannot be sustained over too great a distance, or perhaps not with all the troops since the strongest will arrive long before the other -- tired and ready to be defeated by an alert enemy.

Use local guides and be familiar with the terrain before sending an army into hostile territory. Use drums and flags because shouts and waved arms cannot signal over the required distances. Fight when the enemy is fatigued or has lost its spirit after using delaying tactics.

In some situations, a victory cannot be won, and therefore battle should not be waged. The general must weigh the advantages and disadvantages of the situation. Even in bad situations, it should be possible to harm or distract the enemy…enough to permit your escape.

He states that a general with any of these character faults should be considered a dangerous liability:

- Recklessness
- Cowardice
- Quick-tempered
- Thin-skinned and easily shamed
- Over concerned for the comfort of the army at the expense of strategic goals

MANEUVERING THE ARMY

Choose the right terrain. Stay in valleys where there is water; camp on hills (but not mountains). Cross the river and keep going; if the enemy pursues, attack them when only half of their troops have finished crossing. Avoid salt marshes; if unavoidable, protect the rear with a thicket of trees. On fairly level ground, let the enemy try to attack from below and keep a line of retreat to higher ground.

Keep troops healthy by camping on dry ground. Don't ford rivers when they are flooding. Avoid natural traps, such as narrow canyons or bogs. Trick the enemy into going into bad terrain. If the terrain is good for setting an ambush, check first that the enemy is not already there.

Judge the enemy's intentions and thwart them. If they try to provoke an attack, for example, stay in a defensible position.

Watch for natural signs, such as birds suddenly flying upwards or dust rising in the distance. In fact, the pattern of the dust indicates whether a line of chariots or a massive infantry division is being mobilized. When birds land, it means that the enemy's camp has been abandoned.

Watch for behavioral clues. An offer with generous peace terms suggests a covert attack is being prepared. If the troops who are sent to collect water, take a drink themselves before filling the tanks, and then the enemy is thirsty. Lavish rewards and severe discipline both mean that morale is low. By contrast, the wise general first gains the confidence of the troops, then drills and trains them.

CONFIGURATIONS OF TERRAIN

The six types of terrain - and the best methods for using them are:

1. Accessible ground with roads:
- Be careful to maintain supply lines.
2. Entangled ground, with tall grasses or thickets:
- Attack is possible from here.
- Retreat back here will be difficult, so think carefully before making that attack.
3. Defensible ground, where it would be better to defer fighting:
- Try to entice the opponent into attacking.
4. Narrow passes where ambushes are likely:
- Get there first and set the ambush.
- Only attack in such a position when the enemy has few troops.
5. Cliffs where options are limited:
- Again, get there first and make it a defensible

position.

• Otherwise, entice the enemy away.

6. Any position far from the enemy:

• It is foolish to make a long march and immediately attack.

SIX FAILURES OF COMMAND

1. Desertion from battle: If the troops are commanded to fight an obviously superior force, they will desert.

2. Insubordination: If the front-line troops are too "strong" and the officers too "weak," then insubordination will result in their desertion.

3. Collapse: If the front-line troops are too "weak" and the officers too "strong" then the troops will be pushed beyond their capabilities. The army will collapse.

4. Ruin: This is the result of officers attacking without waiting for orders.

5. Disorganization: If orders are unclear and there are no regular duties, then the army is disorganized. Again, this is disastrous.

6. Rout: If the general sends weak troops against a strong enemy, without regard for morale and leadership, then his army will be routed.

Sun Zi claimed that the terrain advantages are more important than the weather, but a great general must also calculate distances and numeric odds. Sun Zi also advised the ruler not to interfere with battle decisions; the general must decide when to attack in order to win.

The general must balance firm discipline with taking the best care of the soldiers. The general must know both his own army's condition and that of the enemy, in order to choose the best time to attack. The general should make calculated planning before moving; attacking is the key to success.

NINE TERRAINS

Despite having discussed six types of ground in the previous chapter, this chapter addresses nine more.

1.   Dispersive ground: Fighting on home soil allows troops with low morale to "disperse" to their homes. This might be the same as "desertion", or perhaps the soldiers simply will not rally to fight with the desperate fury that Sun Zi wants.
•   Concentrate on maintaining morale.
•   Do not initiate an attack.
2.   Facile (or "easy") ground: After only making a short advance into enemy territory, it is too easy to retreat. Others have suggested that the general must burn the bridges behind his own army, to eliminate the option of retreat.
•   Keep the army close together, to minimize the chance of desertion.
•   Do not stop here; keep advancing.
3.   Contentious ground that is valuable enough to dispute:
•   If either or both sides consider this territory to be valuable, then it is worth contending.
•   Again, keep the army together or ensure that the flanks and tail meet up with the head.
•   Surprisingly, do not attack here; the enemy probably is ready to defend and has strong reasons to do so.
4.   Open ground:

47

- Either side can travel over this territory easily.
- Be vigilant against enemy attacks.
- Allow the enemy to move, since attempts to hinder them will be futile and open the possibility of counter-attacks.

5. Ground with intersecting highways; more specifically, where several realms meet:
- Controlling this territory allows the general to press the neighbors to become allies.
- Therefore, do make allies.

6. Serious ground:
- The situation is "serious" if the army has penetrated the enemy's territory but hasn't managed to secure its supply lines or hasn't pacified all of the territory to its rear.
- Sun Zi strongly recommends gathering supplies as the army may become mired in this position. Apparently some later commentators suggest that the invading army should also build good relationships with the local enemies, by treating them as humanely as possible.

7. Difficult ground:
- Any terrain that is difficult to traverse: mountains, dense forests, swamps, etc.
- Keep moving; do not set up camp.

8. Hemmed-in ground:
- Narrow canyons, deep rivers or high mountains are dangerous, since the army might be ambushed or simply penned in.
- Escape by whatever stratagem might work, but do not allow the troops to desert.

9. Desperate ground:
- Like hemmed-in ground, but with immediate danger

from the enemy: the only option is to fight in desperation.
• Fight in desperation; tell troops that the situation is desperate so fighting without reservation is their only hope.

Sun Zi also recommends throwing the enemy into disarray. For example, attack directly when there is something to be gained. Attack the flanks and the rear in order to disrupt communications. Seize or threaten some valuable asset to draw the enemy away from prepared positions. Move quickly when the enemy is unprepared.

Make the army desperate, by placing them in desperate situations with no clear escape route and then even out the strengths and weaknesses of the troops: put the weakest or most fearful troops on the most advantageous ground so all will remain fighting to the end.

Keep secrets from the soldiers to deceive the enemy, who no doubt has spies. Get information. What do potential allies want? What is the local terrain? What does the enemy want? Play along until a trap can be set.

INCENDIARY ATTACKS

Sun Zi suggests five types of incendiary attacks:
1. Attack the enemy's camp to burn their soldiers.
2. Burn the enemy's infrastructure supplies, such as food or fuel.
3. Burn the enemy's transportation, literally their supply wagons.
4. Burn the enemy's weapons and their ammunition.
5. Burn the enemy in their battle lines or in their camp

Such attacks require the right ammunition and supplies, as well as the right weather conditions (dry and windy). The main advantage is the surprise and disarray of the enemy; without that, it is pointless to press the attack. Have the wind at the back before starting a fire, so it does not spread toward the army.

Releasing a flood on an enemy is more difficult and less useful than using fire, but one should consider using it as an alternative.

Only move or attack when one can gain an advantage, but do not hesitate when the opportunity arises. Do not attack simply out of anger.

EMPLOYING SPIES

Sun Zi highlights the huge expense of warfare, especially as it may drag on for years, causing high taxes and misery for the common people. He concludes that spending relatively minor sums on spies is the only humane course of action because spying is the only way to gain the information required to gain advantage and win swiftly.

THE FIVE KINDS OF SPIES ARE:

1. Local spies: civilians who live in the targeted region.
2. Inward spies, who are close to the powerful people, or within the politics or bureaucracy, of the targeted region:
•   These include those with failing careers or those more greedy than loyal.
3. Converted spies: there are two types:

• Those who deceive spies known to be loyal to the enemy with false information.
• Those who heavily bribe known spies and pay them to lie to the enemy.
4. Doomed spies: give false information to our own spies; allow them to be captured so they will divulge falsehoods under torture.
5. Surviving spies: these are the "regular" spies who covertly learn from the enemy and report back to us.

Spies are valuable assets, but must be well treated and rewarded for what they do. It is especially important to convert spies away from the enemy because they can help find local and inward spies. Previously, Sun Zi had stressed the need for superior knowledge in order to gain tactical advantage over the enemy. The use of spies is the primary method for gaining that knowledge.

SUMMARIZING "THE ART OF WAR"

"The Art of War" contains many lessons that apply to either armed conflict or economic competition. Sun Zi, of course, explicitly discussed armed conflict. His main points include:
• The importance of leadership for morale as well as for superior information and planning.
• The need to compete where one has an advantage, even if that advantage is the desperation of having no alternatives.
• The need for timing: planning ahead; training and preparing; waiting for the opportunity; then seizing it.
• The need for superior knowledge: knowing the

landscape; knowing the enemy's strengths and weaknesses, and providing false clues to mislead the enemy.

• Warfare is expensive. Therefore, plan carefully; employ spies in order to gain the "information advantage"; act swiftly after making the preparations.

APPLYING THE "ART OF WAR" TO ECONOMIC COMPETITION

Several lessons for business leaders arise from "The Art of War", including:

1. Match the leaders to the front-line employees.
2. Sales managers must understand how to motivate people-oriented sales personnel, for example, and IT executives must know how to manage detail-oriented technical staff.
3. There is a need for the "information advantage".
4. Does your firm engage in market research? Is it more accurate or effective than the research performed by your competitors? If not, how can you make it so?
5. Do you "mine" your own IT systems for patterns? When do sales increase or decrease? Do some supplier's cause problems due to poor quality supplies?
6. Competition is expensive. Therefore plan and prepare before acting swiftly and resolutely.
7. For example, small price reductions may lead to a "war" of attrition, but a significant price reduction plus a major marketing campaign may drive increased volume of sales before the

competition can react and recover.

8. Another requirement for this strategy to succeed is to cultivate customer loyalty on a basis other than the low price, assuming you do not want to remain the low-cost alternative forever.
9. Maintain and build morale: ensure the employees are well-compensated in return for meeting the high demands placed upon them.
10. Understand what builds morale for different types of people or different departments.
11. Be consistent in soliciting and responding to employee feedback.

Most of Sun Zi's ideas can be adapted to the business world, especially when compared to other Chinese philosophies, and we will return to this analysis in chapter 11, however, there is a case to answer as to whether China is currently adopting Sun Zi's policy of aggression against its neighbors in the South China Sea.

IS SUN ZI CASTING A SHADOW OVER THE SOUTH CHINA SEA?

With their own wars dominating the headlines, the western world has been largely oblivious to the fact that China has been flexing its military muscle against some of its poorer neighbors in recent years, as a long-standing dispute with Vietnam and the Philippines over two chains of islands: Paracels and Spratlys, threaten to escalate disproportionately.

Why would China be bothered about these islands? Well,

in true Sun Zi style, China definitely has the military advantage, and not only is China vehement in its assertion that it has a claim on the islands stretching back two millennia, but crucially, the islands are surrounded by vast, largely untapped natural resources and China as well its neighbors who also lay claim to the territory, are stepping up the rhetoric, in what, if it continues could turn out eventually to be a pretty ugly confrontation which totally flies in the face of the exemplary examples laid down by Zheng He, and has all the hallmarks of the military genius, Sun Zi.

5. CO-EXISTENCE: CONFUCIUS AND FAMILY ORIENTATED RELATIONSHIPS

THE LIFE AND INFLUENCE OF CONFUCIUS

With Sun Zi, still casting his shadow over the South China Seas, even after all of this time, I would like to pause to reflect upon the life and teachings of one of his contemporaries, Confucius. Both men lived during what was undoubtedly a time of great change and transformation in Chinese culture. Not just a philosopher, he was also an intelligent speaker; his words have echoed down through history. For a warrior, the change moved from the importance of chivalry in combat to the need for victory by any means. For a bureaucrat, it was a change from hereditary entitlement to employment and promotion based on merit.

As Sun Zi embodied the pre-eminent requirement for victory, so Confucius was the example of the importance of merit over birthright. His father was in the "noble warrior" class of society but died when Confucius was only about three years old. Therefore, his family did not have much wealth. Life was a struggle for the young Confucius, but he was determined to make his mark on history. In fact, Confucius is the perfect example of how a person can succeed no matter what class of society – or amount of wealth – they have. His career began slowly, with a variety of menial occupations before he became a successful bureaucrat and, eventually, Justice Minister for the state of Lu. He resigned after deciding that his Duke was not worthy of his service. Confucius then travelled and taught.

THE PHILOSOPHY OF CONFUCIUS

Since the late 6th century BCE, Confucius's strongly influenced Eastern philosophical, cultural, and legal systems have led millions of people in the Path to Enlightenment. He taught that people can improve to near perfection by dint of effort in both personal and interpersonal dimensions. He also taught that a person should strive to be morally virtuous. Since it would be impossible to survey all of Confucianism, this book will focus on his three concepts:

• "Ren": reciprocity, the Golden Rule, "Heavenly Mandate" to govern or lead
• "Li": ritual, the 5 Relationships (the central focus for this chapter)
• "Yi": righteousness, an internal moral compass

REN: RECIPROCITY

The key statement for Ren is that a person should "Do not do unto others what you would not have them do unto you." This is almost identical to the Golden Rule attributed to Jesus in the Bible. "Therefore, all things whatsoever ye would that men should do to you, do ye even so to them" (Matt. 7:12, King James Version). "And as ye would that men should do to you, do ye also to them likewise" (Luke 6:31, KJV).

Confucius advocated Ren as a way for people to behave "humanely": to treat one another with civility, simply incorporating Ren into your life can help you to become a better person and in turn, get better treatment.

There was a political dimension to his teaching, as well. At the time, a political leader had autocratic powers over others, but a ruler with disregard for Ren would treat his subjects in an inhumane manner. His subjects would be nothing more than slaves, rather than, living human beings. Confucius foresaw that his subjects would then be inhumane toward each other. Following a mystical phrase, the ruler might lose the "mandate of Heaven" that he had received before he became the ruler. From a practical viewpoint, his subjects might rebel, or at least, not fight as vigorously as they may have done otherwise to defend their inhumane ruler. In contrast, a benevolent ruler would likely be obeyed willingly and completely; the people would reciprocate their ruler's benevolence with their loyalty.

Other examples of reciprocity involve family and social relationships. Confucius strongly believed that family ties are extremely important. The relationship of parent to child is similar to that of the political ruler to the subject. Perhaps the exception for Confucius was the peer-to-peer relationship between friends.

LI: RITUAL

Confucius extended the notion of "ritual" from a prescribed act that was purely religious, to include all polite and proper interactions among people in society. These are the "routines" that people follow and are not necessarily formalized.

Confucius differentiated between ignorant but correct

behaviors based on poorly-understood legal enforcement versus intentional, well-understood and self-actualized actions. For Confucius, a person should know the correct things to do and should want to do them.

To some degree, Li includes all culture-driven behaviors as rituals. He says we should wear clothes appropriate to the occasion; mind your manners while eating; be loyal and unselfish in relationship to family, friends, and society – these are all rituals.

Some see Ren as "inward" or personal, but Li is definitely "outward." Certainly one must demonstrate Li in body language and actions; just as certainly, Confucius expected that a part of learning Li requires "academic" study.

Like Ren, Li also has implications in the political realm. Confucius judged rulers worthy or unworthy based on their adherence to Li. Also, if people did internalize these ritual behaviors and follow them, there would be no need for legal enforcement through punishment.

YI: RIGHTEOUSNESS

While Li always refers to external, visible actions that conform to societal norms, Yi refers to actions that truly are correct or "righteous". There is a moral imperative to do the right things because they are right. It may not be in one's selfish interests to follow Yi; indeed, it may cause undesirable consequences for others as well as one's self.

Following Yi might lead to conflict with Li, as found in the following example. If I learn that my father has stolen something, Li leads me to inform the authorities, but Yi impels me to honor my ties to my father and remain silent. In this case, Confucius would say that the family obligation outweighs the societal: I should honor my father by not informing the authorities. Yi always trumps Li.

Confucius believed that people intuitively know Yi but need to work at behaving correctly; there are temptations to act selfishly. The principle of Ren should inform one of what is Yi: seeking reciprocity should indicate what is righteous.

RELATIONSHIPS FORM THE CIRCLE

Confucius saw these virtuous concepts as tied together in relationships. Often referenced as "filial piety", or the reverence a son has to his father, there are five types of bonds between:
1. Ruler with governed,
2. Father with son,
3. Husband with wife,
4. Older brother with younger brother, and
5. Friend with friend.

Confucius believed each of the first four to be hierarchical. For example, the ruler governs the people, and the people obey their ruler, but there is a relationship nonetheless. Only "friend with friend" qualified as a relationship between equals.

These relationships require special examples of Ren and Li, which are not found elsewhere. We have already mentioned that the ruler should behave benevolently so that those governed will obey wholeheartedly. There are parallel reciprocal duties and actions required in each of these relationships.

At the very heart of Confucius's philosophies was the belief that family is paramount over everything else. He also wrote a lot about the need for children to be respectful to their elders, as well as ancestor worship (Honoring the dead) As time goes on, it becomes inevitable that we are going to suffer the loss of someone close to us; grandparents are followed by parents, and eventually we lose our husband or our wife. Grief affects people in many ways, but by remembering those that we loved, and reminiscing about the good times that we shared, can help with the healing process, even if it doesn't ease the immediate pain of the loss.

In Western societies in particular, Confucius's notion of a wife being respectful, and by default, obedient to her husband is definitely outdated and in February 2013, The Office of National Statistics in Britain, released data which showed that it is estimated that 42% of marriages in England and Wales end in divorce and there has been a boom in the amount of couples attending marriage counseling in recent years. The fact that couples are willing to seek help shows that there is a desire to preserve their marriage. Maybe if more people took the time to study Confucius and his teachings, and choose to honor his teachings in a contemporary manner then a lot of heartache as well as costly counseling and divorces could be averted. For example, if a husband and wife agree to be mutually loyal and respectful then not only does this bode well for the longevity and success of their union, but it also sets an amazing example for their children, who in turn if they come from a home in which both their mother and father are valued and respected in equal measure, will then find it easier to be respectful to their parents and their elders.

6. FOUR OTHER CHINESE PHILOSOPHIES

INTRODUCTION

Even a brief survey of Chinese wisdom would be incomplete without a passing reference to these philosophers – yet alone an entire book. For this reason, I am mentioning them:

• Lao Tzu and the Tao Te Ching
• Tao Zhu Gong, the practical philosopher of retail Marketing
• The I Ching (Book of Changes)
• Zhuge Liang (The memoirs of dispatching the troops)

LAO TZU

Lao Tzu (or "Laozi", "Lao Tse", or many other transliterations) is credited as being the author of the Tao Te Ching. Scholars debate whether one person known as Lao Tzu truly existed, or whether "he" is a myth or represents a blend of philosophers. This chapter deals with Lao Tzu as if he were a person. Since the words "Lao Tzu" mean "Old Master," it is probable that this was the honorific title for the person, rather than his actual birth name.

Lao Tzu lived in the sixth century BCE, either as a contemporary of, or briefly before, Sun Zi and Confucius. He may have been a scholar or historian ("Keeper of the Archives") in "the royal court of Zhou." One story says that, as Lao Tzu traveled west to leave

China, a border sentry recognized him and asked him to record his wisdom: thus the Tao Te Ching was written.

LAO TZU, THE TAO TE CHING AND DAOISM

The name "Tao Te Ching" may be translated as "the classic (book) [ching] way [tao] of virtue (or power) [te]". In China, this book is often called "Laozi" for its author. The modern Pinyin transliteration is "Daodejing."

The book is central to both the philosophy and religion of Daoism and has influenced other Chinese philosophies and religions. It consists of 81 short but cryptic poems. One concept is that "nothing" can be the most important thing: "We piece doors and windows to make a house, and it is on these places where there is nothing that the usefulness of the house depends."

Another philosophy is that a leader might best achieve results by apparent inaction: That when his task is accomplished, his work done, throughout the country everyone says, "It happened of its own accord."

As an ethical philosophy, Daoism has "Three Jewels," which are followed: compassion, moderation, and humility. As a broader philosophy, a central Daoist concept is "wu wei," which is: "action through inaction" or "effortless effort." This is highlighted by a story about Confucius being corrected by Lao Tzu. Confucius complained that he had worked hard to share his philosophy of personal improvement by striving for

"Ren, Li, and Yi"; but few rulers were willing to work at following these precepts.

"Good", replied Lao Tzu. "You, too, should cease striving".

Whereas Daoism may be seen as a religion, Lao Tzu is seen as the incarnation of one of the three god figures, the "Three Pure Ones". Although these deities represent pure cosmic energy, they are pictured as three older men, each with his own color scheme. Lao Tzu's divine avatar, Taishang Laojun, is the one pictured with an all-white beard. Each deity is closely associated with his own heavenly realm and divine energy.

A Confucian view of Tao might state that the "Way" should be followed by exercising one's personal morality. Daoists might say that the "Way" is spontaneous and most easily followed by not resisting the direction in which the universe is trying to guide humanity.

Westerners have a tendency to neglect the philosophy of "Te" of the "Tao Te Ching" in its aspects of power and virtue. A combination of Tao and Te are considered most closely related to the Hindu concept of Dharma, which is the impersonal natural law that guides moral actions. However, the Chinese expect that the results may be seen in the present life, whereas Hindus expect Dharma to be made manifest through reincarnation.

Daoism is concerned with balancing Yin and Yang, the

female and male principles that include the concepts of inaction and action. Indeed, when the Tao Te Ching turns to discussing Te, it begins with:

The man of highest "power" does not reveal himself as a possessor of "power"; therefore, he keeps his "power." The man of inferior "power" cannot rid it of the appearance of "power"; therefore, he is in truth without "power.'

Perhaps Sun Zi would agree on this view of combat: the best fighters do not make open displays of wrath. The greatest conqueror wins without joining issue; the best user of men acts as though he were their inferior. This is called the power that comes of not contending. Sun Zi might consider the use of such tactics as a praiseworthy act of intentional deception, where Lao Tzu would see it as honest and natural.

Sun Zi might agree more fully with another Daoist, Zhuangzi, who said, "When a man has perfect virtue, fire cannot burn him, water cannot drown him…I mean that he distinguishes between safety and danger, contents himself with fortune or misfortune, And is cautious in his comings and goings. Therefore, nothing can harm him."

Sun Zi might espouse the need for preparation and self-knowledge, but advise that recklessness is sometimes required to make the army fight with desperation.

TAO ZHU GONG AND RETAIL PHILOSOPHY

Born as Fan Li, he renamed himself Tao Zhu Gong after

successfully advising his king, Goujian of Yue, in both politics and war. Tao Zhu Gong then pursued a career in business. By selling pharmaceuticals, he achieved great wealth. In the legend, he also retired to live on a boat with Xi Shi, a woman famed for her beauty. Folk tales may have based the god of Prosperity on stories about Tao Zhu Gong. It is reported that Tao Zhu Gong also advised that wealth is a means to an end, and should be discarded if it becomes burdensome.

Tao Zhu is known for his Twelve Golden Rules and Twelve Golden Safeguards. The Rules are often stated as follows:

1.   Pay attention to people to determine their character;

2.   Handle people without pre-judging them (as prospective customers);

3.   Maintain your focus on your business and personal goals; don't play around with your future;

4.   Stay organized, or at least appear to be well-organized, to attract business;

5.   Adapt to changing circumstances; this too requires being well-organized;

6.   Manage receivables: collect what is owed to you;

7.   Manage employees for their best performance;

8.   Market your business by educating your customers;

9.   Buy inventory shrewdly.

10.   Seize marketing opportunities (Tao Zhu Gong was one of the earliest proponents of SWOT analysis:

Strengths; Weaknesses; Opportunities; Threats);

11.   Lead by example, by following your own standards and enforcing them among employees; and

12.   Understand the business cycle and marketing trends.

The Safeguards are expressed as pieces of "Do not do this…" advice -

1.   Do not be so efficient that it is inhumane or stingy;

2.   Do not procrastinate; rather, seize opportunities boldly;

3.   Do not make a show of your wealth;

4.   Don't lie; instead, be truthful in your business dealings;

5.   Don't delay collecting on debts, which are owed to you;

6.   Don't initiate price wars, at least without careful planning done first;

7.   Don't follow fads; instead, ensure that they are long-term trends;

8.   Don't fight the business cycles; rather, time the natural rise and fall of supply, demand and prices;

9.   Don't cling to the status quo; instead, stay informed about making progress;

10.   Don't overextend yourself by buying on credit;

11.   Don't deplete your reserves; and

12.   Don't endorse products blindly; instead, check their quality and the procedures, which are being used.

THE I CHING

Some claim that the "Book of Changes" is the foundation of all Chinese wisdom. The original "I Ching" or "Book of Changes" is also attributed to have been written by Fu Xi, who was supposed to have received supernatural inspiration when he compiled this tome. Also known as Fu Hsi, Fu Xi is a personage of mythic status in Chinese pre-history. He is said to be the "first of the Three Sovereigns", and is credited with inventing fishing, trapping, cooking and writing.

The book is also known as "Zhou I," which means the "Changes of Zhou," which reflected upon the name of one of the earliest known versions. Confucius consulted the I Ching, as did Lao Tzu and many others. This book played a key role in the founding of the Zhou dynasty in 1070 BCE.

The I Ching is usually explained as a set of 64 hexagram patterns. Each pattern has six rows, either a long unbroken line or a pair of short broken lines. The user randomly selects a pattern by throwing yarrow sticks or dice.

Each hexagram is composed of two trigrams: the top trigram has the top three rows; the bottom trigram has the three lower rows. Each of the eight possible trigrams has its own meaning, and each pair of trigrams creates a more complete meaning. When the user properly casts for an "I Ching divination" and properly interprets the meaning, then the user will have a good understanding of the right course of action.

The various trigrams include concepts such as yin ("yielding earth," which meant life and nourishment in late summer) and yang (which meant "heaven" and "strength" in late autumn); thunder in the springtime; water in the winter; a mountain in early spring; wind or wood in late spring; the sun, fire and lightning in the summer; and a lake in the autumn.

While the ancient Chinese philosophers had some similarities, they had differences, as well. Tao Zhu focused on how war and business was similar. Whereas, Confucius was more focused on loving others – he believed love was war; war against the darkness, Finally, Sun Zi taught how one could deceive the enemy to gain the upper-hand. While these philosophers all contributed to modern Chinese beliefs, the differences are very noticeable. War has been approached quite differently in Chinese philosophies which has helped its society to flourish,

The I Ching was studied extensively among the intelligentsia during ancient times and captured the imagination of several of the dynasties. It is widely believed that Confucius wrote numerous commentaries on the meaning of the I Ching.

You don't need to study the I Ching too hard to be able to apply its sacred messages to your everyday life. There are extensive resources online for those wishing to dissect it fully, however, at a glance here are just a few ways in which the text can be used by those wishing to seek enrichment through a transformational path.

The First Hexagram (The Creative) – Is about using your creative skills to your advantage. This could be applied to work or academic life, or simply embracing your creativity to enjoy quality time with your family.

The Eighth Hexagram (Grouping) – This symbolizes a coming together, a union and could be studied further to enhance relationships either with your partner/spouse, or for strengthening and deepening friendships.

The Twenty-Fourth Hexagram (Return) – Could symbolize you returning to your childhood home or town, or could herald the return of a much loved child from university or their travels.

The Twenty-Eighth Hexagram (Great Preponderance) – This is about stretching yourself and exceeding personal expectations by reaching for the stars and over-achieving.

I have outlined just four examples. The I Ching offers unlimited possibilities for those willing to embrace it.

ZHUGE LIANG

Zhuge Liang, sometimes known as Kongming was born around 300/350 years after Sun Zi and comparisons are frequently drawn between the pair. Born in Yangdu,

Langya, which is the present day Yinan, Shangdong was orphaned and raised primarily by his uncle. An intellectual, Liang enjoyed a close friendship with Liu Bei, a warlord and founder of the state of Shu Han during what was known as the Three Kingdoms Period. A respected diplomat, like Sun Zi, Liang was also renowned for his logistics and military planning skills.

Following Liu Bei's death, his son Liu Shan and staying true to his father's last wishes, he appointed Zhuge Liang, Marquis of Wu. Soon afterward, Liang was also appointed as Governor of Yi Provence, with responsibility for all state affairs. Rather than engage in bloody battles, Liang would always try to respond to provocation with diplomacy, preferring to use violence as a last resort, and in this respect he can be compared to Zheng He.

His primary objective was to restore the Han dynasty. Concerned that local tribes might try to stage a revolution, by advancing into the capital Chengdu, while he was dealing with their arch-enemy, Cao Wei in the North, rather than wage war, he launched a diplomatic charm offensive on the South, enabling him to launch his Northern campaigns without fear of further internal unrest.

While preparing for his offensive on the North, Liang wrote his famous Chu Shi Biao (Dispatching the troops) and unlike "The Art of War" which documented detailed strategies for going to war, The Chui Shi Biao, was a meticulous and well thought out justification for the mission, and in it, he advocated fairness in rewards and punishment, as well as the promotion of talented officers. Liang launched a total of five campaigns against the North, during which time due to his skills as a planner, his forces never suffered more than 5% in casualties. He was also incredibly frugal, ensuring that he achieved maximum gains on a limited budget. In 231 BC, Liang went head to head with the newly appointed commander of the Wei, and during the Battle of Mount Qi, sustained some quite heavy losses. Three years later at the Battle of Wuzhang Plains, Liang fell ill and died in camp.

7. COLLOBORATION: ZHENG HE'S GRAND VOYAGES

EARLY LIFE

Zheng He was born in 1371 in Kunyang, which is the present day Jinning, just south of Kunming; this is located near the southwest corner of Lake Dian in Yunnan. His given name was "Ma He (**馬和** / 马和) indicative of his poor ethnic Hui (Chinese Muslims) family. Ma is the Chinese version of "Mohammad." Zheng He's great-great-great-grandfather, Sayyid Ajjal Shams al-Din Omar, was a Persian governor of Yunnan province under the Mongolian Emperor Kublai Khan, the founder of the Yuan Dynasty which ruled China from 1279 to 1368.

Zheng He was the third child in the family, and his childhood name was Sanbao, which means "three jewels." He had one elder brother, one elder sister and three younger sisters.

Ma He's father and grandfather were both "Hajji," which was the honorific title for Muslim men who made a pilgrimage to Mecca. Their travels to Mecca contributed a great deal to young Ma's education. He grew up speaking Arabic and Chinese. He learned a lot about the western world and its culture. Ma He's father remained loyal to the Yuan Dynasty even though the rebel forces (that would become the Ming Dynasty) conquered increasingly larger territory of China.

During the Ming's conquest of Yunnan and before the defeat of the Northern Yuan, a Ming army was sent to Yunnan to defeat Basalawarmi, the Yuan loyalist. During this time, Ma's father was killed. The Ming army butchered an estimated 60,000 people and castrated the young sons of prisoners – a custom since the first millennium. The eleven-year-old Ma was detained by the Muslim troops of Ming Army. Buo Yu De, the general of the Ming Army was impressed with Ma due to his exotic looks and intelligence. It was said that Ma Sanbao was handsome, tall, and dark with fierce eyes. General Buo sent Ma to Beiping (now Beijing) to the court of Zhu Di , one of emperor's sons, who would later become Yong Le Emperor. At the age of 13, Ma was castrated and made into a "eunuch" [1] and assigned to serve the household of 21-year old Zhu Di.

LIFE IN ZHU DI'S PALACE

During his life at Zhu Di's household, Ma was given excellent education and his needs were provided for. At that time, eunuchs were not trusted by the emperor. They were not trusted with government matters and were not given any responsibility. But Ma He was not like a typical eunuch. Typical eunuchs were emotionally volatile and effeminate. In contrast, Ma He was heavily built and quite tall (he was said to have been seven feet tall). In the military, he developed a reputation for being a brave, intelligent, and commanding soldier. He fought devotedly for Price of Yan when the latter seized the throne and this loyalty gained him the trust and respect of Zhu Di.

When Zhu Di, the young prince, went on a mission to conquer Nanjing in 1402, Ma He served as one of his commanders. Ma He showed his military skills in that battle. Zhu Di usurped the imperial throne of China in 1403 to become Emperor Yong Le. Yong Le continued to follow the policies of his predecessor, Emperor Taizu, with regard to foreign relations. These policies could be summarized as: defend Chinese borders against incursion; maintain peaceful relationships with surrounding nations and encourage foreign trade, including the receipt of tribute from allied nations.

China's most important international commerce included selling tea, spices, silk and ceramics. Trade routes included overland caravans and ocean-going trade. Since ceramics was heavier than spices, these goods were better suited to transportation by ship.

In 1404, when Zhu Di reigned by the name of Yong Le, Ma He was bequeathed the name "Zheng." Thus, Ma He became Zheng He. Then, Zheng He was assigned the position of "Head Eunuch, which was a title as high as the fourth ranked officer.

Seven naval expeditions were sponsored by the Ming Dynasty between 1405 and 1433. The exact reason for these voyages is still a mystery because several official documents relating to Zheng He were burned in the 16th century. But it is believed that the Yong Le emperor devised these expeditions to inflict imperial control over trade affairs, establish a Chinese influence outside China, and make an impression on foreign people in the Indian Ocean basin. It also expanded the Ming Government's tributary system. Some historians have claimed that the voyages were also an opportunity to seek out Zhu Yunwen (the previous emperor who went into exile).

ZHENG HE'S PROLIFIC VOYAGES.

Zheng He went on seven voyages as follows:

1st Expedition(1405–1407) Champa, Java, Palembang, Malacca, Aru, Samudera, Lambri, Ceylon, Kollam, Cochin, Calicut

2nd Expedition **(1407–1409)** Champa, Java, Siam, Cochin, Ceylon

3rd Expedition **(1409–1411)** Champa, Java, Malacca, Sumatra, Ceylon, Quilon, Cochin, Calicut, Siam, Lambri, Kayal, Coimbatore, Puttanpur

4th Expedition **(1413–1415)** Champa, Java, Palembang, Malacca, Sumatra, Ceylon, Cochin, Calicut, Kayal, Pahang, Kelantan, Aru,Lambri, Hormuz, Maldives, Mogadishu, Barawa, Malindi, Aden, Muscat, Dhofar

5th Expedition **(1416–1419)** Champa, Pahang, Java, Malacca, Samudera, Lambri, Ceylon, Sharwayn, Cochin, Calicut, Hormuz, Maldives, Mogadishu, Barawa, Malindi, Aden

6th Expedition   (1421–1422)   Hormuz, East Africa, countries of the Arabian Peninsula

7th Expedition   (1430–1433)   Champa,   Java, Palembang, Malacca, Sumatra, Ceylon, Calicut, Fengtu etc (18 states in total)

Emperor Yong Le set Admiral Zheng He the task of strengthening foreign trade while demonstrating Yong Le's power and emphasizing the legitimacy of his rule. Yong Le wrote a mission statement, including a list of vassal states and foreign countries that Zheng He would visit and a declaration of peace and cooperation with their rulers.

Zheng He had to make meticulous preparations for each voyage. His strategic planning included arranging for large numbers of sailors and huge ships, and carefully considered ports of call. He also had to ensure that those ports would be ready for ships to dock, to make repair facilities available, and to allot land for temporary warehouses. He used specialized ships for different purposes; different types of vessels carried trade goods, horses and personnel.

In the 15th century, travelling on the water depended upon how well the weather held up. Zheng He made use of monsoon winds to power his sails. This required timing the visits and planning layovers when the winds would not blow his way. His voyages typically took two years based on the weather conditions.

He also had to train his staff. Although he was the chief of the diplomatic corps, he sent other ambassadors to reach more ports to maximize China's outreach in the limited time they had for each voyage. Military personnel needed discipline to avoid bullying locals and to give diplomacy a chance to sway foreign leaders. Medics in his fleet were told to treat the ill at their ports of call. As well, navigators and sailors were briefed on the routes and the winds that would prevail during the seasons, and the timing of rendezvous.

He had to remain on top of details and he insisted upon results. In the command of 100 to 200 ships and up to 27,000 people, Zheng He could not afford wasted efforts or delays. A typical visit from Zheng He would include:

• A public proclamation of the Emperor's mission statement;
• Official visits with the local ruler, including an exchange of gifts;
• Medical treatment for the local populace by the fleet's medical cadre; and
• Law enforcement, by means of capturing the pirates who preyed upon either the Chinese or the local traders

THE FIRST VOYAGE

It is probably also worth noting that, at that point in time, China's most important international commerce included selling tea, spices, silk and ceramics. Trade routes included overland caravans and ocean-going trade. Since ceramics were heavier than spices, these goods were better suited to transportation by ship.

Zhu Di suggested expeditions down the Western Ocean as well as the Indian Ocean in 1405, one year after he became the emperor. Zheng He was assigned the Admiral of the voyage.

On July 10, 1405, the crew had a grand feast where Zhu Di wished them good luck and made some sacrifices in the name of Tianfei, whom they worshipped as the sailing Goddess.

On July 11, 1405, Emperor Zhu Di gave a final speech as the mariners prepared for their first voyage. Admiral He wore a long red robe and traditional tall black hat. They had a crew of approximately 27,800, a squadron of 62 treasure ships for living quarters, and 190 supporting ships. There were ships for trading goods, supply ships for staples, water tankers, etc. They said prayers praising the compass and boarded the ships. The captains admired the superb invention. Monks burnt incense to frighten away ghosts and wished for the best. They were determined and already certain to reach places such as Calicut, Taiwan and several Arab countries in the Western Ocean.

First, they reached Champa's town Qui Nhon where they traded rhino horns, elephant trunks and also wood. After reaching Malacca, they traveled onto Cambodia and Java, arriving six weeks later. They then sailed southwest to Ceylon (now Sri Lanka) and Calicut and as the king of Ceylon was ill-mannered, Zheng He immediately left.

The fleet stayed at Calicut for nearly four months from December, 1406 to April, 1407. Zheng He defeated the fleet of pirate Chen Zuyi when they visited Palembang, Sumatra. Chen Zuyi was particularly shrewd and Zheng He eventually prevailed. He took Chen Zuyi back to China to face punishment. This act gave the people of Palembang peace. He appointed a new leader of Palembang and eventually the city became a Chinese ally.

The ships each had a room dedicated to Ma Tsu, the Chinese goddess of the sea as all of the crew members prayed to her every night before dinner. A huge bronze mirror was used to reflect evil spirits when they arrived at new land. The ship carried silk, porcelain, and copper coinage to trade for spices, fragrant wood, gems, animals, textiles and minerals.

During their voyage, they ate brown rice, soya beans, wheat, millet, green beans, limes, lemons, oranges, coconuts, pears, vegetables, frogs, dogs, pigs, and dates. They drank wine and sometimes they drank tea (red or green oolong). So the crew ate healthy foods to maintain a good lifestyle. Living on the ships was hard, but worth it and the crew hugged dogs and pigs as a defense against the cold weather. They sprayed arsenic to prevent insects and had ferocious dogs to scare rats.

The biggest challenge against nature was their miraculous survival during a huge rare storm that hit the ocean. Zheng He arrived at Nanjing in 1407.

Items of trade included silk, porcelain, tea, pepper, women, wood, silver, Ming goods, ginger, textiles, cinnamon, textiles as well as many other kinds of food and goods.

THE SECOND VOYAGE

Although not much information is to be found regarding the second voyage, it is believed that after bringing back wonderful goods from the first voyage, Zhu Di demanded another voyage. The second voyage started sometime between, 1407 and 1409. Their fleet consisted of only 249 ships due to many of the ships from the first voyage being rendered useless. Zheng He revisited many places from the first voyage. This time, they traded more in Siam and sent back goods such as peacocks, elephants, parrots, wood, and tin. The fleet also visited Calicut again.

THE THIRD VOYAGE

In the fall of 1409, Zheng He and his crew set sail again. Taiping was their first stop and then Champa ten days later, before sailing onto Malaysia, Singapore, and Malacca. In Malacca, Zheng He traded aloe tree, ebony, and dammar tree. After trading in Quilon, Cochin, and Calicut, they arrived in Ceylon. Zheng He returned from the voyage on June 16, 1411, again laden with fine goods.

THE FOURTH VOYAGE

In December 1412, Zhu Di ordered a fourth expedition. This expedition was the largest yet with more than 28,000 men in tow. The fleet took off in January 2014 and was destined for Hormuz. Zheng He hired Ma Huan as the chief raconteur of the voyages. The first fleet, led by Zheng He, went to the Maldives and many other kingdoms. The second fleet, led by Yang Min – another commander under Zheng He, went to Bengal.

The fact that Zheng He was a courageous leader was proven again in this voyage. Although Zheng He always tried to exhibit diplomacy and peacekeeping, a contemporary reported that Zheng He "walked like a tiger" and did not avoid violence when he considered it necessary to impress foreign people with China's military might and Zheng He captured Sekander, a notorious outlaw in Semudera, as a show of strength, and to set an example of how enemies would be punished. They traded coconut trees, shells, rubies, diamonds, amber, pearls, and carpets in Semudera. From the other side, Yang Min brought with him an extraordinary gift in the form of a giraffe. The giraffe was brought from Malindi, Kenya on Sep-20, 1414. It was believed to be a "quilin" – which is a mystical creature. The fleet returned home in the summer of 1415.

THE FIFTH VOYAGE

After Zhu Di had constructed the Forbidden City, Zhu Di ordered a fifth expedition and this time the fleet targeted not only the Western Ocean and Arab Peninsula but also Africa. First, they traded goods such as paintings and other artistic products at Quanzhou, before moving onto Aden where they traded gemstones, bracelets, jewels, and rings. The reception in Aden was apparently particularly warm, and Zheng He was welcomed very warmly at

Aden, where they paid tribute to the Yong Le Empire with Zebras and Leopards.

From Aden, the fleet of Zheng He went to Mogadishu; their first African country. Hereafter, they went to Brawa (Somalia) and Kenya, where they traded perfumes, glasses, and carpets.

Zheng He was a diplomatic leader and each of his military experiences proved this further. He could have destroyed and blown away the resistance that the people of Mogadishu exerted. But instead, Zheng He used subtle tactics by explaining to them the vision of Yong Le Dynasty and traded gifts. This worked, and they surrendered to the Admiral. Zheng He returned home on July 15, 1419.

THE SIXTH VOYAGE

On February 2, 1421, officers gathered in the newly created Forbidden City. Qilins were brought to celebrate, and everybody was happy. Everything was going well for the Yong Le emperor, but the celebrations would not last long.

Suzhou's Madame Wang was Zhu Di's favorite concubine who died shortly after the ceremony. In the spring, an accident occurred while the emperor was hunting. The horse was ill, and Zhu Di was very angry. Soon, lightning struck the Forbidden City. Fires burned many places and halls. Zhu Di received criticism and was mad. He started to become ill. On August 12, 1424, Zhu Di, the much loved Yong Le emperor, passed away.

Zheng He did not attend the funeral, because he and his crew were sailing. There is very little information available about this voyage as all the focus at the time was on Zhu Di's death. The only information that is available was that in November 1421; Zheng He instantly returned due to the emperor's death, and this is where the widespread belief that it was the rest of the fleet that visited America, the Cape of Good Hope, and circumnavigated the world, stems from.

THE SEVENTH VOYAGE

Before Zhu Zhanji, Zhu Gaozhi was emperor. But his reign and life did not last long. Months after he was crowned emperor, he passed away. After Zhu Di's death, his grandson, Zhu Zhanji, succeeded him, as he had always admired his grandson's intelligence. In 1426, Zhanji, at the age of 26, became the fourth emperor of the Ming dynasty. Zhanji never paid much attention to Zheng He, but finally on June 29, 1430, the emperor ordered a seventh and final voyage. The voyages were only for trade between Siam and several other appointed kingdoms.

On January 19, 1431, the fleet departed for the final time. They went to their usual destinations – Vietnam, Malacca, and Malaysia. They also arrived in Calicut on December 10, 1432. The fleet also split up. Hong Bao led the voyage to Hormuz.

On the return voyage, Zheng He fell ill. He died at the age of 62, and his family said "…A life at sea should die at sea." According to religious tradition, he was buried at sea. Wrapped in white cloth, his body, was thrown into the sea with chants by sailors saying "Allah is great". Zheng He's passing marked the end of voyages which had spanned twenty-eight years.

ZHENG HE AND THE PIRATES

I have already touched upon briefly, one of Zheng He's encounters with a pirate. Piracy was a major problem for Emperor Yong Le, just as it is today in the horn of Africa. Indeed, the young emperor was so concerned about the marauding bands of pirates that were wreaking havoc, and harming the interests of his political allies or vassals, that he tasked Admiral Zheng He with eradicating the problem, and by ruthlessly ridding the waters of these pirates, particularly at the Strait of Malacca, Zheng He created safe passage through the straits, as well as, increased China's status in Southeast Asia.

Zheng He was careful to maintain good relations both with local rulers and the emperor while performing his policing duties. He had to avoid antagonizing locals or harming innocent bystanders. Had Zheng He dealt with the pirates without first gaining the approval of local rulers, his police actions could have been seen as aggression against them.

After Zheng He arrested the pirates, he sent them to Yong Le so that righteous justice could be served. The politically-savvy Zheng He allowed Yong Le the honor of carrying out the justice that they saw was fitting for the pirates.

ZHENG HE'S LEGACY IN CHINA

Zheng He was arguably China's greatest transformation expert. He was not as much a philosopher as he was a practical over-achiever, and preferred to teach by example more than by his writings. In an age where China could easily have played the role of aggressor on the international stage, Zheng He's approach was diplomatic and collaborative.

Although He was a great success in his voyages, it may be said that his immediate legacy was found in the far flung countries that he visited rather than at home in China, for Yong Le's son chose to shun international trade and diplomacy, favoring a policy of isolationism, which subsequent emperors, would continue for the next five centuries.

In recent decades, Chinese political leaders and historians have begun to praise Zheng He's achievements more than ever before. Perhaps his achievements have become a useful example particularly at this time when China has begun to open its borders to trade and has started to exert its influence in the world. After all, Zheng He was known for his focus on diplomacy and didn't lord his position over anybody. He viewed all leaders as strong and willingly united with most of the leaders he met.

ZHENG HE'S LEGACY ELSEWHERE

Monuments to Zheng He are found in several of the countries he had visited in his grand voyages. In some cases, these commemorated the benefits of trade and medical treatment which Zheng He had delivered.

Another reason these countries celebrated Admiral Zheng He's visits is that he represented "soft" Chinese diplomacy rather than "hard" military power.

Admiral Zheng He's contributions to Chinese philosophy may be listed as:
- Collaborative Efforts and Delegation of Tasks
- Soft Power: Trade and Commerce
- Consolidate, Rather than Explore
- Meticulous Planning

CONSOLIDATE, RATHER THAN EXPLORE

Admiral Zheng He tended to stay "on the beaten track". Emperor Yong Le set Zheng He's itinerary with a view to consolidating China's influence with its known allies and neighbors and although he frequently travelled aboard, Zheng He was happy to trade with established partners and did not seek out new countries or markets.

The simplicity of Zheng He's voyages was apparent in the map of his travels. He did not attempt to explore unknown countries. China was familiar with the majority of countries surrounding the Indian Ocean, and had been, for centuries, a primary producer and consumer of goods trading among the Mediterranean, African, and Middle Eastern regions.

METICULOUS PLANNING

Perhaps Zheng He was conscious of following Sun Zi's advice from The Art of War, in planning his voyages as carefully as any general might plan a military campaign. Among the considerations for Zheng He were:

1. What gifts would be appropriate for the local rulers?
2. What trade goods would be required, and in what quantities?
3. What livestock would be needed?
4. How much food, medicine and forage would be needed for the voyage?
5. Knowing the winds shift seasonally, could they arrive at a safe port where they could wait for the next opportunity to travel?
6. Do they have the personnel to do all the work, including diplomats, sailors, soldiers, craftsmen, and laborers?
7. Are they trained and also instructed in what to do and how to do it?

Meticulous planning is essential when crafting a business strategy and I will draw further conclusions from Zheng He's voyages in subsequent chapters.

8. ZHENG HE: A PARADIGM FOR MODERN TRANSFORMATIONAL LEADERS

Although economic success in modern China is due, in part, to the accumulation of wisdom from its ancient philosophers, I would argue that Zheng He best represents the transformational leader required in the modern world. I also make a comparison of Zheng He with other ancient Chinese wise men in the area of transformational leadership and why Zheng He comes ahead of the pack.

WIN-LOSE OR WIN-WIN: THE ART OF WAR VERSUS ADMIRAL ZHENG HE

Sun Zi's Art of War has a significant following, and his principles remain sound when one is engaged in all-out, winner-take-all warfare. In modern business terms, this would be a zero-sum game, like poker, where one party's winnings result directly from another's losses.

First, Sun Zi and some European armies in the Middle Ages could plunder the countryside to replenish their supplies. They did so with impunity, because there was no concern for making willing allies of their current enemies. Today's armed conflicts require a more delicate touch. All the recent multi-national military action in the Middle East has been concerned with "winning the hearts and minds" of the locals.

Second, Sun Zi had no remedy for the case where a general recognized that his Emperor was pursuing a misguided war. In a modern democracy, a government is not allowed to pursue a course of action without an occasional mandate from the people.

Finally, as mentioned, Sun Zi advocated win-lose strategies, but modern business requires ever-shifting alliances and the pursuit of win-win situations. One example may be found in the field of mobile telephone technology. Hardware manufacturers, software companies, independent application developers, and ringtone content providers depend on one another to develop and maintain market share, while competing with each other to share the revenue.

We see more win-lose situations in Western history which is tainted by the "conquistadors" and the colonization of the Americas, among others. These were not seen as opportunities to develop commercial relationships among equals and were certainly detrimental to the aboriginals. Indeed, the Thirteen Colonies rebelled against England when they felt their former countrymen were exploiting them economically.

In contrast, Zheng He provided an excellent example of pursuing "win-win" situations in fostering mutually beneficial trade relations. His mandate was not to bludgeon China's vassal states or weaker neighbors.

OUTMODED CONFUCIAN RELATIONSHIPS

Perhaps the greatest improvement that Confucius suggested was that we become more polite to other people, and more respectful of their opinions and their right to a peaceful life.

However, it is difficult to apply the entire world view that Confucius held dear. We choose our governing representatives rather than accept hereditary emperors. We expect to examine government policies and decisions as well as the personal shortcomings of our elected politicians.

While family ties are important and may be treated more carefully, we do not hold to hierarchical relationships for life. The "duty" of wife to husband, son to father or younger sibling to older is more egalitarian than vassal to lord. There are literatures that criticize the use of Confucian philosophies in business particularly its support of using family members to run family businesses. Modern corporations require the best brains and talents to stay competitive which may be found wanting among family members.

He served the emperors as they appointed him to his missions. In his role as admiral, he did indeed command his fleet, including sailors, soldiers, merchants, and diplomats. However, we can take note of Zheng He's accomplishments and learn from his methods without accepting the full cultural baggage that is inherent in Confucianism. Rather, Zheng He is a model of a strong leader commissioned to fulfil a task. Next, we discuss other ancient wise men and how they stack up against Zheng He in the area of transformational leadership.

STRIVING TO REACH LAO TZU'S STANDARDS IN THE TAO TE CHING

It has been argued that Lao Tzu's Tao Te Ching could easily be either an interesting philosophy, or a true religion. It does, however, take time and effort to learn and master an approach that abstains from effort and creates results with effortless striving. It is also difficult to balance action and inaction, or "male and female principles", within oneself except by immersion in this philosophy. A modern Western view is that each of us should express their own personality. Some may live in the Daoist balance more naturally than others with more gender-specific modes of behavior.

It may be healthy and wise for a stereotyped "hard-driven business executive" to step back, relax, and allow their subordinates to work out details on their own. It may be difficult for a board of directors to appreciate this approach in the face of shareholder demands for quarterly growth in revenues and earnings.

Zheng He, by contrast, gave clear direction. He made careful plans in terms of itinerary, cargo and agenda, but wasn't afraid to delegate tasks as circumstances required. Since he could not personally meet with every dignitary or ruler, he sent diplomats on their own missions. This systematic delegation and trust were both effective and efficient.

TAO ZHU GONG AND RETAIL PHILOSOPHY

Since Tao Zhu Gong is beyond criticism as a consultant for retailers but Gong's advice is useful for making limited improvements to an established enterprise. He cannot "transform" an outmoded business model into a new paradigm.

THE I CHING

The I Ching is like the Tao Te Ching and Daoism: the "Book of Changes" requires significant effort to understand and even more to apply wisely in everyday life. It also goes against Western rationalism to believe that an act of divination can provide better guidance than rational analysis. Zheng He may have consulted the I Ching, but his plans and actions were rational and explicable.

ZHUGE LIANG

Zhuge Liang's strategies were similar to Sun Zi, which were used very much in military to deceive the enemy. It was not a win-win approach and therefore did not come out as attempts made to transform the enterprise or organization.

ZHENG HE AS A MODERN TRANSFORMATIONAL LEADER

With so many corporations and countries in turmoil and

decline, it is useful to carefully consider Zheng He's guidance on being a transformational leader.

PROCESS, RESULTS, INNOVATION, INSPIRATION

Admiral Zheng He did the careful planning for the logistics of his expeditions. He chose the routes, ports, and gifts and trade goods that were to be transported. As chief diplomat, he was most responsible for strengthening alliances and ensuring good relations with those he visited. He was a sufficiently inspirational leader that he kept the loyalty and obedience of his men through long voyages. How did he accomplish successful trade across seas? He used a variety of tactics: transparency, collaboration, a drive toward win-win situations, and generosity.

TRANSPARENCY

In the modern world, social media makes journalists of almost everyone; and these journalists are not advised by corporate lawyers or reined in by editors. Every thought, every action, is laid bare and open to the world for ridicule and scrutiny. Therefore it is imperative that business leaders must be seen to be ethical and to be available to respond quickly in times of crisis. An ill-timed or insensitive comment these days is the equivalent of corporate suicide as social media sites like Facebook and Twitter expose so much of our lives and a sense of public accountability that there is no margin for error.

COLLABORATION

Do modern corporations follow Admiral Zheng He in finding win-win collaborations and partnerships? In the technology space, collaboration has been a fruitful strategy. Mobile telephones represent one type of opportunity, where a software company such as Google can partner with a handset manufacturer like Motorola. Application developers for cell phones sell their products through virtual stores operated by major players, even if the application competes with the manufacturer's product. A similar example of cooperation is evident if one sources computer hardware from HP but asks for Oracle database software to be installed. Even if these two companies are sometimes rivals, they must also work together.

THE DRIVE TOWARDS WIN-WIN SITUATIONS

A modern win-win situation is exemplified in open-source software and open systems. Open systems are developed and supported by corporations as well as individuals. While there are obvious competitive advantages to owning and controlling an entire operating system, the open system approach can also be attractive.

Consider the Android telephone. By using open systems, the cost of development is shared by many collaborators. The product can reach its market sooner and at lower cost: two of the major factors in building a competitive advantage over rivals. Each collaborator gains by having their product move forward into the marketplace.

Some people also prefer open-source products to proprietary systems. Whether or not this market segment is worthwhile on its own, it does provide a group of vocal supporters who will promote the product in their blogs and to their social networks.

He worked hard to ensure win-win situations. Rather than exploiting trade opportunities to maximize short-term profits, his goal was to build long-term trading relationships by providing value in each transaction.

To return to our example, we can see that Android and cell phone manufacturers have a lot to learn from Admiral Zheng He. It's true they have come up with an advantageous relationship in order to compete with the Apple iPhone and iPad. However, while Android developers may not have been remiss in providing updates to their operating system, manufacturers have been slow to adapt and distribute these upgrades to their customers. The unfortunate result is that Android now has a reputation for being slow to update software and fix software bugs. This is obviously not the right way to build a long-term relationship with consumers or with a business partner.

Apple, likewise, has recently released the non-upgradable, non-hackable, and non-fixable iteration of the Macbook Pro. The iPad and Macbook Air are both characterized in the same way, but consumers happily bought into them. The Macbook Pro, however, is a different product that has been known for its power, upgradeability, and decent resale value. So where previously, Apple consumers were happy not only with the sleek designs of Apple laptops but also with their longevity, this latest version has a definite limited lifespan and once done with, will have virtually no resale value; even with advanced technology such as a retina display. With the popularity of Samsung's Galaxy smartphone range, it will be interesting to see whether Apple's marketing and advertising strategies will continue to prevail over a product that is now less advantageous to consumers and actually bad for the environment. Considering what looks like the future forced obsolescence of Apple products, this runs counter to the whole idea of building long-term relationships by providing value in each transaction because the value itself has been diminished, and the focus has become the selling of a lifestyle.

GENEROSITY AND FREE SAMPLES

One of Zheng He's most compassionate acts, when visiting foreign countries, was to send his fleet's medical staff to treat locals in the port cities where they stayed, before lavishing gifts upon his hosts.

While free samples have long been a marketing staple, it is increasingly important to provide a sample or other benefit to promote one's business, at least in some areas. Will a transformational leader find it useful in a particular industry?

Every organization can provide some free but useful information through their corporation website. A construction company's site might include a blog page with reminders about job site safety procedures or what to consider when buying materials. This information should be related to the company's business and areas of expertise, but also be useful even to non-customers.

Corporate generosity is also a way to build good will and gain valuable publicity. Some have found that employees bond as a team when performing charity work on company time. Habitat for Humanity is a not-for-profit organization that builds homes for deserving families. They use volunteer labor, including teams from local businesses and the home's recipients also contribute "sweat equity," working on their own homes; they also pay enough to keep Habitat for Humanity solvent. As this particular organization becomes known and respected for its efforts, the companies who send in build teams on special occasions are reported in local news media.

9. CORPORATE TRANSFORMATION METHODOLOGY

I am going to start with a modern transformational leader Jack Welch, who is famed for transforming General Electric. He turned it around from a moribund company beset with internal competition and slavish obedience to outdated processes and procedures, into a dynamic hotbed of invention and innovation. One reason for his success was that he challenged and changed the corporate culture. He encouraged and rewarded success, but replaced the least productive sales staff annually. He also mellowed down his style from a Neutron Jack in the earlier years of his career to Transformational Jack, following the footsteps of Zheng He's art of collaboration.

While ancient Chinese philosophers such as Zheng He, may not have had modern day corporate giants in mind, when they were philosophizing about ways to improve the world, savvy CEO's have taken their wisdom and devised clever corporate transformation techniques, to turn around companies facing financial difficulties.

To illustrate the corporate transformation process, I would like to use a three-phase approach which may be compared to treating a patient who needs surgery, resuscitation and therapy and I will demonstrate not only how the teachings of Zheng He, Sun Zi and Confucius have been developed in this manner, but also how Jack Welch ran with them to transform G.E. Before I do this, it is, however, important that we understand what the three phase process is.

PHASE ONE: SURGERY

The surgical phase is undergone to restructure the company to face harsh new realities. This phase involves cutting costs, improving operational efficiency, and seeking a quick increase in cash flow. This may involve reducing headcount, replacing first-class airline flights with conference calls, or selling outdated goods at a discount (and terminating warehouse leases). This phase is "ruthless" since the corporation's continued existence is at stake.

However, it must not be mindless cost-cutting and improving operational efficiency; it must also prepare the way for the next phases. This phase requires a surgeon with a scalpel, not a butcher with a cleaver or swordsman with a broadsword. It is not a slash and burn exercise but rather calls for the surgeon's skill.

Just as a surgeon needs a team of nurses and doctors the turnaround executive needs to have a team to implement the strategy and to assist in communicating the strategy for their employees. In fact, communication is vital in managing the negative emotions surrounding layoffs or cutbacks. Timely and transparent communications can raise morale since people will rally around a forthright leader who promises and delivers decisive action.

Furthermore, a doctor does not delegate the task of delivering important information to a nurse to inform the patient; the doctor speaks directly with the patient. So although the management team has a role in communications, the turnaround executive must deliver the top-level news directly to the organization.

PHASE TWO: RESUSCITATION

The resuscitation phase is deployed to revitalize revenues and profits. It seeks new markets and new sources of revenue. This phase must set and achieve the short-term goal of returning to profitability. It must balance the cost-cutting from the first phase with the need for expanding market reach and sales revenues.

Some modern corporations are beginning to learn to use digital social media. Even for companies that are not formally going through corporate turnaround, the learning process is like experiencing a resuscitation phase. Facebook and Twitter, whether mediated by computers or smart phones, call for historically new degrees of honesty, openness, transparency, and collaboration with customers. Just one example will suffice: a hotel chain learned of a bedbug incident because a visitor used Twitter to complain to friends.

Companies must establish an online presence to monitor complaints and deliver their own message. The companies must then be quick to respond and be honest in their dealings. Customers will provide feedback; how will the company respond to harsh criticism read by, potentially, hundreds or thousands of interested bystanders?

In terms of marketing, traditional media is saturated and often mistrusted. Building relationships with customers via two-way digital media, like Facebook and Twitter, is one avenue where customers may be found. Another path is to co-brand or co-operate, as found in the alliances between software companies and mobile telephone manufacturers. Microsoft and Google battle each other using Nokia, Samsung, HTC, and others as partners.

PHASE THREE: THERAPY

The therapy phase involves rehabilitating a strong and healthy corporate culture. It consolidates previous gains by instilling a new corporate culture that seeks and adapts to new challenges. This phase may introduce revenue sharing or continuous improvement programs; it may seek new ways for employees to cooperate rather than compete. During this phase, the corporate leader must look toward the future and plan for the long-term viability and growth sustainability of the company. This is a phase to build a strong corporate immune culture. In medical science, we understand that the best way to fight viruses is to build a strong immune system. In a corporation, the strong corporate immune system is the corporate culture that is fast, flexible, and innovative.

The therapy stage is somewhat like the East's view of traditional Chinese herbal medicine, which seeks to balance and regulate the flow of energy in the body. Western medicine, by contrast, uses drugs to treat specific ailments, often by killing germs. Herbal medicine often takes a longer view, seeking to strengthen the patient by improving internal harmony. Corporate "therapy" must take a long-term view for sustainable growth.

Phase one and, to some extent, phase two, sit very well with the western medical system, which is ideal for treating acute diseases. Phase three runs parallel to Chinese traditional medicine, which is used, even to this day, in the treatment of chronic diseases.

In contrast to autocratic monarchs, or "lone wolf" chief executives, Zheng He employed collaboration even when seeking a goal with single-minded determination. In the following chapters, I will explore how the three phase techniques can be applied to his teachings, as well as the teachings of Sun Zi and Confucius, before looking more closely at how Jack Welch, the former CEO of General Electric, successfully used collaborative efforts to bring GE to greater heights, some six 600 years later.

10. LESSONS FROM ZHENG HE ON CORPORATE TRANSFORMATION

ZHENG HE AS A ROLE MODEL FOR MODERN CHINA

It is not surprising that the second largest economy in the world: modern-day China has continued to adopt Zheng He's strategic diplomacy and willingness to explore new terrain. Modern Chinese economics seems to follow Zheng He's game plan by returning to international Asian markets. China has extended its reach, seeking raw materials from Africa and North America. In addition, China now permits her people to spend money abroad as tourists.

ZHENG HE AS AN EXAMPLE FOR CORPORATE TRANSFORMATION

He was not a business executive, saving a corporation from bankruptcy. He did, however, use many of the techniques espoused by the Corporate Transformation in its three phases of surgery, resuscitation, and therapy. The following is a summary of the practices for transformation that he used.

Although Corporate Transformation does progress from one stage to the next, Zheng He used the techniques at different times and according to his immediate circumstances and needs. Zheng He also used a more collaborative style than would be expected whether for his times or modern times. The table below highlights the salient approaches of Zheng He in accordance to the three phased corporate transformation methodology.

CASE STUDY 1 – ZHENG HE AND THE THREE PHASES

	Surgery	Resuscitation	Therapy
Operation	Preparation Law Enforcement	Salesmanship Customer First	Positive Trade Cross Cultural Relations
Strategy	Carefully select countries to visit Build (Shipyards)	Public Relations Build more Infrastructure (Warehouses)	Plan for future Bring foreign people home
Culture	Increase Commerce Avoid War	Develop Friendly Relationships Adventurism	Empower workers Medical care for foreign people

ZHENG HE AND SURGERY TECHNIQUES

To use "Surgery" techniques requires a leader who is bold and resolute. Clear directions must be given, and the leader must ensure that orders are carried out. The situation requires decisive measures, because failure in this stage spells the end of the mission. Zheng He used "Surgery" techniques in two ways: in preparation and law enforcement.

THE SURGERY OF PREPARATION

Serious, careful, and meticulous planning is required to sail a fleet of over a hundred vessels. Trade goods, provisions, and labor are obvious prerequisites, but so are plans for the weather; ports for layovers and repairs; and temporary warehouses.

Even more in the fifteenth-century than today, ocean travel depended on the weather. He made use of monsoon winds to power his sails. This required timing the visits and planning on layovers when the winds would not blow his way. His voyages typically took two years, based on the weather conditions.

As one example of staffing: the fleet employed one medic for every 150 or so sailors and staff personnel. As already mentioned, the medical team treated the masses at each port of call, as part of Zheng He's diplomatic overtures.

Admiral He and the emperor also ensured that he had a team of high-level envoys. With the right staff available, he could leverage his abilities. This is an obvious parallel to the way of a surgeon who leads the surgical team: an anesthesiologist, anesthetist, scrub nurse, circulating nurse, etc.

Zheng He had to keep a relentless focus while preparing for each voyage. He had to remain on top of details and to insist on results. In the command of up to 27,000 people, Zheng He could not afford wasted efforts or delays.

In such a large operation, delegation of authority and responsibility is paramount for success. He led his team by giving them opportunities to learn, to take responsibility, and to make preparations for their roles in the voyages.

Emperor Yong Le had, in fact, prepared the way for Zheng He by sending out a reconnaissance voyage two years before Zheng He's first. No doubt that learned from and improved upon, the Emperor's preparations for that mission.

Zheng He also used a continuous improvement process. He deliberately found ways to improve his team's operational efficiency after each voyage. This was especially important because many of his men were soldiers, medics, or diplomats, and not sailors. As an example, his first voyage did not visit nearly as many countries as subsequent voyages. They learned from the first voyage and applied those lessons to the later ones.

THE SURGERY OF LAW ENFORCEMENT

It is essential to note that Admiral He was careful to maintain good relations, both with the local rulers and with the emperor while performing his policing duties. He had to avoid antagonizing the locals or harming innocent bystanders. Like any CEO, he had to ensure that the Chairman had the final verdict in dealing with captured pirates. In collaborating with his Emperor and with the local authorities, Zheng He advanced his primary mission of fostering good will and respect for the Chinese among the people he visited.

In both roles, as a planner and as an agent of law enforcement, Zheng He demonstrated a corporate surgeon's precision in planning details, clarity of instruction to subordinates and resolute diligence in acting.

ZHENG HE AND RESUSCITATION TECHNIQUES

"Resuscitation" shifts the focus from the immediate to the medium term. It builds on past success from the "Surgery" phase. In a corporate setting, cash flow is still critical, however building the future cannot come at the expense of current revenue.

Clearly Zheng He was a master of resuscitation techniques, as shown in five areas: developing markets; expert salesmanship; public relations; serving customers' interests and making investments.

RESUSCITATION THROUGH DEVELOPING MARKETS

He "developed a new business" by going to his "customers." He found new opportunities by strengthening old ties with neighboring countries. This push for new and expanded markets is in keeping with the corporate resuscitation phase.

A major part of his work could be considered "resuscitation." It did look to the past, since an element of the mission was to remind the neighboring states that they needed to maintain friendly relations with China. Although he definitely expended most of his effort in expanding commerce with markets that were already known to the Chinese, he was expanding China's economic reach by changing these neighbors from quiet bystanders into active trading partners.

RESUSCITATION THROUGH EXPERT SALESMANSHIP

On his fourth mission, for example, Zheng He took 63 ships and over 27,000 men to the Maldives, Hormuz, and Aden. As a result of this journey, nineteen countries sent return missions to the Ming capital at Nanking, a real coup for him, in terms of market development. Zheng accompanied the representatives of these missions back to their home countries as part of his fifth expedition.

This was a significant act of cooperation and support. His naval capabilities were superior to those of the countries he visited. Zheng He had to coordinate these foreign vessels along with his own fleet, expanding his effort, but making the trip much safer for his allies.

RESUSCITATION THROUGH PUBLIC RELATIONS

Whenever Zheng He dealt directly with agents from different countries or cultures, he would have been very aware of the public relations role he was taking on. He was representing the Emperor at all times, and in essence, was acting as a salesman for China: he was selling the goodwill and culture of his home country, intending that the host country would "buy" what was on offer and open trade relations with China.

RESUSCITATION THROUGH SERVING CUSTOMERS' INTERESTS

All those actions contributed to Zheng He's resuscitation techniques. He eliminated territorial struggles by providing a conduit for envoys from neighboring countries to visit China and return home safely. This was a clear instance of integrated diversity and countries sharing a common vision: the value of maintaining friendly and open trade relationships. Taking action to further their joint interests was another example of the collaborative spirit Zheng He brought to all these dealings.

RESUSCITATION THROUGH MAKING INVESTMENTS

His missions did require a significant investment from the Chinese in building the ships and facilities such as warehouses and shipyards. However, Zheng He had an obligation to "make a profit" during his voyages, in terms of building goodwill, earning respect, and of course, making money in commercial trade. In this sense, Zheng He was involved in the "Resuscitation" phase. He was building toward the future while still making it pay off during the present.

ZHENG HE AND THERAPY TECHNIQUES

In Corporate Transformation, the "Therapy" phase begins to develop a new mindset and a new corporate culture. These are essential for the long-term growth of the company, although they will not, by themselves, save the company from bankruptcy. The "Therapy" phase requires a more collaborative leadership style than the one used in "Surgery."

Zheng He provided therapy by using creative innovation and planning for sustainable growth. He empowered his subordinates, spread good will, and planned for the future. However, the main intent was to change other countries, not the Chinese themselves. His goal was to improve China's standing among the other countries, by demonstrating good faith and cooperation. It was incidental that his work could have led to further changes among the Chinese, had later Emperors followed the path of Emperor Yong Le.

THERAPY BY EMPOWERING SUBORDINATES

Admiral He developed and commanded a large fleet. Zheng He delegated diplomatic missions, arranged for later rendezvous, and coordinated their efforts. This is similar to the way a manager at any level might provide growth opportunities for his or her direct reports. This is a clear example of empowering his "employees." The advantage of this empowerment is the upgrading of an employee's attitude and performance as they take "ownership" of their responsibilities and duties. Another bonus to empowerment is the increase of innovation and creativity from an individual. When one feels free to work on their own, there is a freedom in how they relate to the company or employer. This freedom often results in a surge of creativity, a plus for the company, and certainly, a large benefit to the employee

THERAPY BY SPREADING GOOD WILL

Zheng He could have used military might to impress and influence his foreign neighbors, instead he chose the soft power of trade and by restraining his fleet from military action, Zheng He was beginning to change the attitudes of foreign leaders.

Although the policy of developing trading partnerships was not new in China, Zheng He did work hard to persuade foreign leaders to adopt this mindset. This is like the corporate therapy phase that fosters change in one's own corporate culture. A very specific example was making the Chinese medics available to as many people as possible in each port of call. This demonstrated that the Chinese had something to offer, even beyond trading goods.

THERAPY BY PLANNING FOR THE FUTURE

The above actions are like building a new corporate culture. The other aspect of the therapy stage of the three-phase transformation program is to make long-term plans and initiate actions to make these plans a reality. Zheng He worked toward this goal, by concentrating his later voyages not on law enforcement, but on the continuation of the new trade relations that were in place. Zheng He was obviously aware that maintaining the good will that had been established during his earlier voyages was as important as law enforcement, perhaps even more important. People like to feel as though they are important and are partners in a relationship, rather than subjects that need to be ruled with an iron fist. This may have continued indefinitely and sustained long term growth, but before Zheng He could start out on his seventh voyage, Emperor Yong Le died, and the next emperor changed the strategic direction for China.

Five centuries later, the new Chinese aspiration to become a significant player in the global economy may be traced back to Zheng He's voyages. Modern China is generating good will and investing heavily in Africa and Latin America, helping the troubled European countries with sovereign debt problems and sending Chinese tourists all over the world including its erstwhile enemy Taiwan. China even extended a helping hand to quake-stricken Japan, though there were diplomatic rows for a short period of time. It is winning the good will of the world through spreading economic good will. This is contrary to the US, which is bogged down with, and has generated a lot of problems through, military incursions into Iraq and Afghanistan.

11. JACK WELCH'S LESSONS IN CORPORATE TRANSFORMATION

In the early 1980s, General Electric Corporation (GE) applied corporate transformation techniques to transform itself into an economic powerhouse. GE was already large, but it required serious and lasting changes. Jack Welch became Chairman and CEO in 1981 and began making those changes. Born in Massachusetts, in the United States of America, Jack Welch is of Irish/American descent. He is a perfect example of how by embracing the methods which Zheng He used for opening up trade to China, and adopting the corporate transformation strategy, Western business leaders can leapfrog ahead of the competition and preside over forward thinking enterprises which are not only fit for purpose, but perfectly positioned to maximize upon the plethora of business opportunities continually opening up, courtesy of the world wide web. A summary of the corporate transformation strategies used by Jack Welch is shown in the table below.

CASE STUDY 2: USE OF THREE PHASES BY GENERAL ELECTRIC

	Surgery	Resuscitation	Therapy
Operation	De-layering	Eliminate turf wars	Product development

	Dismantle "Financial Mafia" More with less	No boundaries Best practices (six sigma)	Innovation with less New systems
Strategy	No 1 or 2 High growth Shrink HQ Strategic planning	Integrated diversity Cross-Functional teamwork	Empowerment: Decision making at lower levels Reward flexibility
Culture	Simplicity Fire bottom 5%	Shared vision and values Work out	360 degree appraisal Crotonville – GE Way

GE'S SURGERY PHASE: OPERATIONAL PRODUCTIVITY

Perhaps the most daring change Welch introduced at GE was to "de-layer" the company. He had long believed that its many layers of management fostered bureaucratic timidity rather than innovation and productivity. Part of that bureaucracy was a "financial mafia" that controlled spending so tightly that it choked reinvestment. Decreasing the layers of management bureaucracy allowed for more freedom to reinvest. Welch also reduced inventory levels dramatically.

GE's new strategy was to become either number one or two in any given market, or to exit that market altogether.

The company sold off divisions that did not lead their markets. This reduced staff and simplified the corporate structure. Welch focused on high growth while shrinking the head office division.

The staff learned to accept that low-performing employees would lose their jobs. The target was about a five percent annual dismissal rate. Another cultural change was that simplicity would eventually triumph over bureaucracy.

By shedding both low-performing employees and uncompetitive divisions, Welch demonstrated the intense, ruthless focus on cost-saving measures that are characteristic of the Surgery phase.

Yong Le had set Zheng He the task of strengthening foreign trade while demonstrating Yong Le's power and emphasizing the legitimacy of his rule, including defeating the pirate chief, Chen Zuyi, in order to maintain order along maritime routes. Admiral Zheng He amassed a huge fleet and made his plans with strict attention to detail. Zheng He ensured that his armada would be well-prepared, and also well-disciplined so as to execute the Emperor's orders. Zheng He had three methods to guarantee the success of his tasks. Like Jack Welch of GE, Zheng He focused upon three main principles:
- Simplicity;
- The goal to become number one; and
- Strategic planning.

Zheng He endeavored to become number one at what he

did. With the Emperor's financial and ideological support, plus his own military acumen, it is not difficult to understand how he became the legend of the sea, a distinction that still holds true today.

His strategic planning included arranging for large numbers of sailors, huge ships, and carefully premeditated ports of call. This meticulous planning was critical in making all of his voyages overwhelmingly successful.

One other tool, which was used by Zheng He, was his recognition of his men, as well as other cultures and people as legitimate in their own right. He respected the men under his command, and, in turn received their respect. There would be no other way to command up to 27,000 men over an immense armada of ships. Likewise, his esteem and reverence for the foreign societies that he visited helped to make China (and Zheng He, himself) a popular, yet formidable force.

By undertaking a long-range approach, Zheng He prepared the way for numerous journeys that would become as successful as his first. The characteristic shared by Zheng He and Jack Welch was the demonstration of laser-like focus and intensity during the early stages of their tenure as the top leaders of their organizations.

GE'S RESUSCITATION PHASE: PRODUCTIVITY WITH INNOVATION

GE's resuscitation phase began a turn toward innovation. Product innovation was made possible by eliminating "turf wars" between divisions. The company began to eliminate internal boundaries. Divisions shared knowledge on best practices, such as Six Sigma and work-out.

GE's strategy shifted toward integrated diversity in its teams and products. Cross-functioning teamwork meant that people with various skills and backgrounds would work together on a project, rather than reviewing and criticizing other divisions' projects.

Welch pushed the corporation to pursue common goals, rather than allowing each division to focus on success for itself at the expense of others.

In addition to his medical team, Admiral He's fleet also included specialists in languages, commerce, construction, and of course, sailing. These cross-function teams were essential for communication with the people they visited. Zheng He knew that the Chinese would have to buy and sell, to build warehouses, and to safely travel from place to place, and the most productive way for this to happen was by establishing distinct political interactions within each destination he visited.

GE's elimination of internal boundaries worked in much the same way. Welch understood that advancement was not possible as long as the company was battling itself internally. He did this by encouraging the pursuit of more efficient practices, including cutting back on inventories and taking apart the bureaucracy that was performing inadequately. As Zheng He learned, Jack Welch also realized that the strength of any company relies upon the individuals that make up its constituency and by encouraging innovation and cooperation within their respective organizations, Zheng He, and Jack Welch were able to successfully communicate and manage those subordinate to them.

GE'S THERAPY PHASE: CONTINUOUS INNOVATION

Welch then pushed GE to adopt a cycle of continuous innovation. Rather than running a product through a "develop, then sell until the competition catches up" timeline, GE would continue improving products or developing replacements. In addition, new systems and methodologies were introduced so GE could innovate more while consuming fewer resources.

Part of the strategy was to empower employees, so decisions could be made further down the corporate ladder. Flexibility, rather than bureaucracy, was rewarded.

Two of the cultural changes were the "360-degree appraisal" and the "Crotonville-GE way." The first involves performance appraisal by peers, subordinates, and customers as well as by managers. The second refers to GE's educational campus, which embodies the goal of life-long learning.

Zheng also "empowered" his diplomatic staff. When he sent them on missions, he trusted that they had the skills to succeed even when he was not present. Of course, they did rendezvous later, so he was kept informed after the missions. These were learning opportunities for his subordinates, who were nonetheless responsible for their missions.

It does seem a pity that his work was not continued by the next Emperor. It would have been interesting to see how Chinese culture could have developed with further cultural and ideological exchange. By turning inward after Zheng He's missions, China was unable to create the major culture shift that GE would experience under the leadership of Jack Welch centuries later. As pointed out earlier, following the death of Emperor Yong Le in 1424, the Ming dynasty temporarily put an end to its attempts to establish subsidiary states and economic partners throughout Southeast Asia. When Emperor Yong Le's grandson ascended the throne, Zheng He began his seventh and final voyage. However, advocates for an isolationist foreign policy held sway, and the funding for Zheng He's enormous undertakings was withdrawn. Rather than utilizing the corporate transformation techniques, China allowed the great strides made by Zheng He to fall by the wayside.

COMPARISON BETWEEN ZHENG HE AND JACK WELCH

Both Zheng He and Jack Welch worked to change their

organizational cultures. Zheng He laid the foundation for future trade and international relations, but China did not follow as explained earlier through for five centuries. Jack Welch succeeded in making the changes he envisioned for the corporate culture at GE, especially in making lifelong learning a key part of an employee's career.

General Electric's corporate transformation under CEO Jack Welch provides a modern perspective on the corporate transformation strategy, and has many parallels to the voyages and deeds of Zheng He during the fifteenth-century. Although "Neutron Jack" started transforming GE with great energy in the 1980s, he did not become "transformational" until later in his tenure. During the first phase, or "surgery," Welch pushed his executive team hard enough that they got into legal trouble for polluting New York's Hudson River and also for skirting financial ethics. During this time, Welch may not have been a match for Zheng He as a diplomat.

Normally the goal of corporate transformation is to save an organization by transforming its mindset and culture. Jack Welch is an excellent example of a leader who transformed his company.

During the resuscitation and therapy stages, Welch became less aggressive. Some executives would disagree with that assessment since Welch broke down the corporate feudal structure where managers would pursue their own goals within their own divisions, at the expense of corporate development. He also dismantled the financial controls that prohibited even worthwhile projects. However, these changes permitted and encouraged collaboration between divisions, a synergy that was of great benefit to the corporation.

"Transformational Jack" emerged towards the end of his career, when he spent a significant amount of time mentoring the next generation of leaders at Crotonville, GE's educational campus. By fostering "the GE way" in passing along the corporate culture to these new managers, Welch more closely emulated Zheng He's development of his diplomatic corps.

Zheng He's mission was to transform the attitude of China's allies and trading partners, rather than to change China's attitudes towards foreigners or about its own politics or culture. Despite this, some of his methods foreshadowed corporate transformation, and his brilliantly collaborative management style can still serve as an example for modern leaders. With this in mind, however, it is important to remember that Zheng He lived more than five centuries ago. Zheng He did not have a formal corporate transformation model to follow. Instead, he put his tremendous spirit into his voyages, combining his military insight with a great humanitarian soul he so obviously possessed.

Zheng He served an emperor who pursued diplomatic relations, peace and prosperity through commerce. He collaborated with foreign leaders. He won their cooperation through honesty and openness. He was a cosmopolitan traveler who was well-acquainted with a variety of different cultures. His religious views may have incorporated Islam.

His focus began from a position of strength. It must have been unsettling for a ruler to see an armada of over one hundred ships arrive for a visit. But even when Zheng He commanded his largest fleet of 200 ships, they did not loot, pillage, or conquer. Indeed, his memory is still honored in a number of those countries, by means of monuments, relics, and historical writings.

12. SUN ZI AND CONFUCIUS ON CORORATE TRANSFORMATION

CORPORATE TRANSFORMATION AND SUN ZI

I have already talked at length about Sun Zi, and how the ideologies that he set down in "The Art of War" have been adopted by world and business leaders for centuries. But how can modern day business leaders, that are hoping to turn around failing businesses, apply the three phases to his philosophies? The table below summarizes the strategies taken by Sun Zi:

CASE STUDY 3: THE USE OF THE THREE PHASES BY SUN ZI

	Surgery	Resuscitation	Therapy
Operation	Win at all costs Right place, right time Quick and clean kill.	Know rivals strengths & weaknesses Develop new products & skills Maintain competitive edge	Lead from the top Be ready for change (Internal & external) Know when to walk away
Strategy	Subterfuge Use of spies	Ensure orders are clear and that staff follow	Earn respect of employees

	Timing is key	them Choose battles wisely Give staff freedom to manage	Be considerate of employees needs
Culture	Stay 1 step ahead Keep staff on toes	Sack underperformers Keep a tight control on finances	High Morale Reward loyalty and hard work with bonuses

The main thing to remember about Sun Zi is that while yes, he was a military strategist and would go to any lengths to secure in a win, including resorting to deception, and the use of spies, he also believed passionately in the need to keep warfare as clean as possible. Modern day business leaders would be wise to follow his example of brutal, decisive leadership in order to avoid complicated and messy takeovers and blood-stained boardrooms. A clinical cull of staff can actually improve morale as well as the prospects for the business' long term survival whereas long drawn out negotiations and indecision, will only lead to resentment and lower output. So, while Sun Zi was engaging in what most Westerners would consider Machiavellian tactics in order to achieve his goals, his contemporary, Confucius was theologizing about how the family is king.

CORPORATE TRANSFORMATION AND CONFUCIUS

Let us next discuss the other famous Chinese

philosopher, Confucius. If Confucius were alive today, then he would be at the cutting edge of corporate social responsibility and he would be a market leader in environmentally friendly, ethical businesses. Business leaders today, seeking inspiration from his teachings with regard to the three stage approach, could maybe look at re-energizing, tired, jaded brands and seek to re-position themselves as innovative, market leaders in their field. They would also be wise to look at his models of reward based upon merit, and seek to introduce family friendly working practices; improving morale, reducing staff turnover and lowering the cost of recruitment in one go. Below is the three phase approach taken by Confucius:

CASE STUDY 4 – THE USE OF THE THREE STAGES BY CONFUCIUS

	Surgery	Resuscitation	Therapy
Operation	Dialogue over aggression Long term vision over short term interests Humane takeovers	Cleanse business of bad practices Good staff training Promote from within	Improve morale Listen to concerns Modest goals
Strategy	Engage competitors ethically	Honest appraisals	Respect competition

	Ethical New Business	Fair prices	Handshake over contract
	Fair contracts	Employees embrace your core values	Respect authority
Culture	Rehabilitation rather than dismissal	Ethical business policies	Reward based upon merit
	Lenience	Profit through good practice	Family friendly policies

DIFFERING APPROACHES: OUTSTANDING RESULTS

They may have been contemporaries; however, in terms of personality and world view Zheng He, Sun Zi and Confucius were poles apart, with each laying the foundations of differing ideologies which would later become the bedrock of the corporate world. In terms of transforming and turning businesses around, it may be more useful to view their philosophies as using ancient techniques under the right circumstances.

While Confucius placed more emphasis on building family orientated relationships, Zheng He, Sun Zi and Welch each applied the techniques of corporate transformation in their own situations. Each achieved spectacular success as leaders in challenging circumstances and led large hierarchical organizations.

All of these men demonstrated that collaboration, teamwork, and cooperation are powerful tools of leadership. Zheng He strengthened alliances with foreign leaders, people who may have distrusted or feared China's might. Jack Welch overturned vested interests inside General Electric, leading to cooperation from aptly-named corporate "divisions." While, in laying down his extraordinary vision in "The Art of War" Sun Zi, unwittingly created a road map, not just for war and how it should be executed, but the business model that has been replicated down the centuries.

The techniques first espoused by all of these transformational leaders can be, and have been, applied in a number of corporations in recent decades. The three-phase corporate transformation program provides a way forward through difficulties to success. Jack Welch has confirmed using the transformational strategies successfully. Zheng He was indeed a great corporate transformation expert and inspiration, and used the transformation strategies much earlier. He had paved the way for the globalization success of modern day China.

13. TRANSFORMATIONAL LEADER: PAST AND PRESENT

THREE ANCIENT CHINESE PHILOSOPHERS

How can we possibly compare and contrast Zheng He, Confucius, Sun Zi and Jack Welch, when three of those men were born before Christ, and the fourth into the twentieth century era of consumerism and capitalism; when given the seismic difference in cultural and societal expectations placed upon them, the methods which they adopted in fulfilling their shared goals, were as different as it is possible to be. Surprisingly, the comparisons and parallels are easier to draw than you might think, for while the ancient Chinese Philosophers were separated more by geography than time, there can be no denying that Jack Welch; an American man, with a Western lifestyle and ideals,   whether by studying the teachings of the ancients, or by simply tapping into and encapsulating the spirit of their philosophies, not only revolutionized corporate America but laid down a blueprint for success.

THE GOALS

Zheng He's mission was set by his Emperor: to "wave the flag" so as to gain increased respect for Imperial China; to improve foreign relations; and to develop trade. Confucius may have been the purest "philosopher" in this group, but his goal was to make interpersonal relationships more effective through harmony and respect. Sun Zi was the consummate general, whose focus was to win war at the lowest possible cost. Ideally, he would rather his Emperor's foes surrender, than waste lives and resources in battles. Confucius was more interested to share certain family values of respect for the elders. Jack Welch's goals were to build a winning organization, by getting rid of bureaucracy and cultivating leaders. Indeed, his primary mantra was "lead more and manage less."

COMMON INTEREST: TRANSFORMATIONAL LEADERSHIP AND MANAGEMENT

Although they used different approaches, the major interest of all of these men was transformation. A different kind of transformation, though in continuity with the other, is found in the philosophy and practices of each of them. Thus, we have four different levels of transformation. Confucius talked about personal psycho-spiritual transformation which developed into a social philosophy and further into a political philosophy. Zheng He focused on socioeconomic transformation which entailed collaborative leadership and management in the areas of trade. Sun Zi focused on political and military transformation. Through the analogy of military strategizing and tactics, he developed a strategic management socioeconomic and political plan. Taken in this context, anyone wishing to bring about transformation in their corporation, must start with the following: creating order from chaos, team building, alignment, calming influence, clarity, and tranquility. Under Welch's sterling stewardship General Electric's profits increased tenfold, and it's revenue fivefold. Since leaving the corporate giant that he turned around, Welch has written a plethora of books, all of which in one way or another are about leadership, and corporate transformation.

PSYCHO-SPIRITUAL AND SOCIAL TRANSFORMATION: CONFUCIAN STYLE

Effective change has to aim at transforming personal attitudes and approaches and the fabric of the society. Thus, Confucius' approach to transformation should be understood at two levels: at the psycho-spiritual level and at the social level. Its aim is the transformation of individuals and therefore easy transformation of the society.

The term "Confucians" means "peaceful" and refers to those who are able to appease and calm others by a certain decent behavior. Confucians became peaceful people as mediators between men and between Heaven and Earth through rituals etiquette. As such, they were specialists in rituals and music and this professional knowledge played an important role in Confucian teaching. Besides, etiquette played an important part in the teachings of the Confucians as a way of making oneself beautiful. This led to a kind of withdrawal and isolationism since they needed constancy as well as the right expertise to discern what is proper and what is not.. From this perspective, Confucianism is often blamed for passivity which made China lose her economic aggressiveness.

However, at the time of Confucius, social comportments,

such as, trustworthiness, seriousness or loyalty had ceased to be observed by the ritual experts, and they had become simple-minded practitioners of rituals without caring much for the social context of etiquette. For Confucius, a ritual expert had to live as an example for others, with high moral standards. For him, the people who were alive were as important as those who were dead. This is what Confucius tried to transform to establish a new way of ordering the society. He stressed benevolent and righteous behavior. For him, a ritual expert could not be but a person of a high moral integrity which is characterized by two virtues, namely, kindheartedness and righteousness. Kindheartedness can be understood as being humane, kind or charitable. In contemporary writings, kindheartedness means to have affection towards someone else or kind behavior. For Confucius, a kindhearted person had to overcome the difference between relatives and non-relatives or between persons standing close in a social network and those standing afar while practicing filial piety which played an important role in his ritual-guided thinking. Indeed, filial piety was the root of kindness which had to be extended to those outside the circle.

Kindheartedness is expressed in a maxim similar to the Kantian categorical imperative which says that benevolence is that "what I dislike should not be done to others." One has to support others if they want to erect or promote themselves; their feelings have to be transferred to others. A kindhearted person uses straight and simple words; she or he loves quietness and longevity, what is immoveable, reliable and constant; she or he is respectful, magnanimous, truthful, diligent and gracious. Kindheartedness is a practical virtue used in daily life and is displayed by giving up the self. The way of the cultivated man is never inclined to one extreme side, but is directed towards the "golden mean" which implies a "well-balanced behavior". It begins at home with filial piety towards the parents and love and respect towards older brothers. It is therefore tied to family relationship. Affection towards other persons ranks only in second place.

In the official sphere, kindheartedness is expressed in two different ways. The first is loyalty towards superiors and the second respect towards others. Loyalty towards superiors is important for the functioning of a state, a smaller polity, or even an enterprise in the widest sense. Filial piety is likewise a crucial constituent for a well-functioning society. Without it, social disorder would erupt. Thus, according to Zeng Shen, who was a disciple of Confucius and a ruler faced with the loyalty of his own ministers and the people had the duty to respond this loyalty with benevolence. This is expressible in the ruler granting to the people what they like such as lowering taxes and using the penal law with caution. He leads the people along the right way by force of his own virtue and makes them feel treated justly by applying the proper rituals. This will, however, raise issues with civil revenues since taxes are the governments' sources of income. This probably accounts for the reason why China, at a certain point, was economically retreating. As far as the use of the penal code is concerned, questions of justice are raised and this, to some extent, contradicts

Confucius maxim of equal treatment.

Kindheartedness can move other people to change their inner heart. It has an educating and exemplarity character that is able to move the hearts of a whole people. In order to become an exemplarity personality, constant cultivation of the self is necessary. In the eyes of Confucius everyone is able to become kindhearted, if one only really wants it. The best way to become a kindhearted person is to give up oneself and to go back to the proper rites. To find the true form of kindheartedness is very easy because it has to be found in oneself.

A kindhearted ruler leads the people by means of virtue and makes them equal by means of rites. Ritual is an expression of righteousness which is characterized by generosity or philanthropy which results from unselfishness in the interaction between persons. "Ritual" is a general term for all rules, regulations, demeanor and customs in different social contexts. Part of rituals originated in religious contexts, when people were communicating with deities, spirits and the souls of ancestors.

When Confucius lived, a lot of nobles disobeyed these ancient prescriptions and rebelled against their lords and masters. Rituals had become vain names and designations. In such a society it was impossible to respect Heaven and to bring sacrifices to the spirits. Without rites it was impossible to give everyone his position in society. The positions of lord and minister, old and young, and husband and wife would be utterly disturbed. Members of the upper and lower nobility indulged in luxury and lacked the sense for an appropriate modesty and frugality. It was therefore necessary to revive the perfect rites established by the Zhou Dynasty.

This is a corruption that is analogous to today's moral and ethical decadence in business, in leadership, and in politics which have basically led to an almost total societal moral decadence. For Confucius, rites were not a meaningless formality but had to be filled with kindheartedness to obtain their full meaning. An outer guideline (li) without an inner spirit (ren) would be useless. Rites without a kindhearted spirit were meaningless, music without a benevolent accent was not beautiful. Yet a personal attitude of kindheartedness without outer guidelines (rites and etiquette) would lead to confusion and chaos. Both had therefore to be combined. Rites were the standard for humankind's behavior, and the latter was the spirit of all ritual behavior. Each and every social encounter that we experience is accompanied by the performance of certain rituals, all seeing, hearing, speaking and doing was involved in etiquette. Rituals were the outer expression of inward kindheartedness; they were the visual and perceivable adornment of a sincere feeling. Rituals therefore played an important role in the private as well as in the political sphere.

Only strict adherence to what the rites of the Zhou prescribed would lead to a stable and peaceful society. The virtuous power of the ruler, combined with the correct sense of sparingly used punishment would offer the population the right sense for what is correct and decent. Politics was to "rule in the correct way" with the help of the ancient rites "to rule a country with the help of rites." A ruler who had rectified his own behavior would be able to bring peace to his country. If a ruler's reign was consolidated with the help of rites then his ministers would serve him with loyalty. If the ruler had cultivated himself, everyone would follow him even without orders, yet a ruler without kindheartedness would not be obeyed even if he decreed orders. Although it is good if the people had sufficient food and a state disposes of a good army, a state whose people do not trust their ruler would never flourish. In a state that is governed by appropriate rituals the ruler was like the polestar around who the people willingly gathered. This could only happen if the ruler gave up himself and returned to the ancient rites, filled with the spirit of kindheartedness and simplicity.

"Yi" (righteousness) is the substance of all activities and as the right manner in which something is performed. It is a kind of behavior "appropriate" to an actual situation. While kindheartedness is mainly reserved in the private sphere, appropriate behavior is applied in the official sphere. The appropriate behavior of the perfect man of virtue is often contrasted with selfishness and the search for profit by the mean man.

The righteous ruler appoints competent and wise talents as his advisors. While the ruler responds to the loyalty and respect of his ministers with kindheartedness, the father answers the filial piety of his son by generosity. Personal moral conduct and behavior inside a family are so directly compared with the situation in a state, and each family was seen as a basic cell of the whole empire. If there was benevolence and kindness, filial piety and generosity inside each family, it would also be found on the level of a state's government. A generous father will incite filial behavior in his son, and a decent and benevolent ruler will make his ministers most loyal not because they are seeking for profit but because they are convinced to serve their lord with their utmost sincerity.

Kindheartedness and righteousness have to be acquired through knowledge and learning. Only a few persons have an innate knowledge. All others have to learn constantly and were only able to achieve their understanding of life by learning; good examples have to be followed and bad ones have to be discarded. Everything one can observe and learn is thus constantly subject to a process of evaluation and of reflection. Learning and reflection about what is learnt, can lead to the way of righteousness. Kindheartedness can be learnt from one's own heart, and there is no way to obstruct those who are willing to learn to become a man of virtue. Confucius knew that it was hard to become a perfect noble, yet there were some points to be observed that at least could lead into the proper direction, namely to study the Classical writings, correct (humankind) behavior, loyalty and trustfulness.

The most important philosopher supporting and expanding the philosophy of Confucius was Meng Ke known as Mengzi. Mengzi (or Mencius, as his name has been latinized) made the rulers a focus of his philosophy and therefore turned Confucianism from a social philosophy to a political philosophy. Benevolence and kindheartedness were to be the right way of government. Only this behavior would contribute to a peaceful society in a state, and in turn to a strong nation that would be able to fend off all foreign challenges; a joyful and content people were the base of a successful government. Confucian scholars would be able to educate rulers, and the latter to have a virtuous effect on their people because the human character was good by nature. Such theories came into being because Confucianists had to cope with a lot of contending schools attempting to bring forward different arguments for the best way of ruling a state. The concept of benevolence seemed not sufficient in the face of institutional reforms that took place in many of the states during the Warring States period. The Confucian philosopher Xun Qing (Xunzi) developed the concept of the necessary implementation of rites (li) to educate the people. Unlike Mengzi, Xunzi defined human nature as bad and claimed that only rituals, like laws (fa), would be able to bring people back to the way of humanity and kindheartedness.

This is important since relations between two persons had become all the more important as status had become less important than abilities. Indeed, Confucianism was, especially among academicians, made liable for China's backwardness during the 20th century. Indeed, while Confucianism could be blamed for "isolationism", it was important in another front. Only with the discarding of socialist ideology in the late 1990s, Confucianism again became prominent as a unifying force of Chinese culture. Confucius transformed the content of their rituals into a social philosophy – a foundation for social transformation through cultural unification.

SOCIO-ECONOMIC TRANSFORMATION

China's economic and industrial production far surpassed all other countries of the world by the 15th century. Except for the remote border regions in Mongolia and Central Asia, peace was restored, and the building and repair of infrastructure-highways, canals, ports and harbors, were under way. Agriculture and manufacturing were advanced, and practical handbooks for production were published and circulated. One of the most useful and practical handbooks was the Tian Gong Kaiwu by Song Yingxing that contained detailed illustrated instructions in manufacturing and crafts based on centuries of experience. A compilation of "all known knowledge of the time" was contained in the encyclopedia, the Yonglo Da Dien (1403-1408). Confucian scholars engaged in academic endeavors and governance. At the same time technological innovations, with practical applications in industry and manufacturing, were vigorously carried out. Systematic and organized production that evolved through centuries was the prevailing intellectual climate of the period. "Doing everything in the correct way and in the proper sequence" was the motto of master shipwrights in Longjiang shipyards. No wonder then 15th century China was the world's foremost producer of consumer goods-foodstuffs, textiles, ceramics, metals especially iron tools, utensils and weapons, paper and lacquer were some of the most coveted trade goods of the world. It stands to reason why China was the dominant world power at the time attracting thousands of foreign diplomats, traders, merchants, religious leaders and scholars. Its large population was also a voracious market for commodities from foreign countries especially from Southeast Asia.

It's time to transform leadership from aggression, confrontation and conflict to collaboration. European superiority, according to Alam (2002), has been put forward with regard to rationality, freedom, individuality, inventiveness, daring, curiosity and tolerance; in turn, these qualities have been translated into superior achievements in technology, wars, management, capitalism, industrialization, and shipping, among others.

CONFUCIAN ISOLATIONIST VERSUS COSMOPOLITAN INTERATIONALIST VIEWS: NEGLECT OF THE SEA-FARING TRADITION.

However astonishing were the accomplishments of Zheng He, the expeditions were denounced by subsequent rulers. When Emperor XuanDe died in 1435, the simmering controversy over the high cost of overseas expeditions and hosting foreign ambassadors surfaced. The Confucian bureaucracy saw only the heavy economic and labor expenditures involved in the expeditions. The mammoth ocean expeditions had long-term detrimental consequences on the people and on the environment. The construction of hundreds of huge ships, shipyards and harbors-including equipping them, providing them with trade goods and supplies, and mobilizing thousands of laborers, artisans and specialists-exacted tremendous toll on natural and human resources. Bear in mind also that in the age when ships were propelled by sail and oars, it was absolutely necessary to obtain large numbers of laborers. Able-bodied male peasants were lured by the promise of material rewards but more often prisoners and innocent men were forcibly conscripted to man the ships. Alongside massive shipbuilding and flourishing overseas trade, slave taking intensified and became more ruthless. The opening up of forests and putting more land under cultivation to raise large amounts of export commercial crops increased the need to obtain labor.

Forests in Jiangsu, Guagdong, Fujian, Sichuan and Annam were decimated to obtain timber and fuel to produce millions of ceramics and metal implements. People not only suffered due to conscription as sailors and shipwrights; onerous quotas on the delivery of materials and products were imposed on them. The system was prone to corruption for eunuchs and local officials in-charge of procurement misappropriated large portions of labor and supplies. Moreover, open and free trade released human proclivity to greed as thousands of eunuchs, officers and sailors took advantage of extracting personal profits from trade and exchanges and avoided remitting taxes and goods to the government.

The Confucian bureaucracy also considered foreign imports as mere "trifling amusements for the court" such as giraffes, zebras, peacocks, scented woods, and perfumes. The fact that the expeditions were led by an eunuch of Mongol-Arab descent and a Muslim was an insult to the scholars who came to office by diligent study and examinations. Fierce rivalry between the Confucian bureaucrats and court eunuchs came to a head, as the latter gained increasing favor and influence on the affairs of the state. Moreover, Confucian scholars viewed Chinese traders overseas and foreign merchants, especially eunuchs, as promoters of political intrigues and economic saboteurs who diverted people's efforts away from the most fundamental economic endeavor that ensured stability of the empire-that of agriculture.

Less than ten years after the expeditions were launched, the Emperor Zhu Gaozhi prohibited overseas travel and trade, halted building and repair of ocean going vessels, and severely punished those who disobeyed. The policy of isolation resulted in tragic consequences. In relinquishing Chinese naval achievements, the government failed to safeguard and defend its coastal borders leaving them easy prey to the predatory brigands and pirates (mostly Japanese) who plundered and devastated entire villages.

By the latter period of the Ming, worsening conditions of the people living on the coast forced many to either flee inland or venture overseas. China's isolationist foreign policy combined with neglect of naval military defense and retreat from international overseas trade coincided with the expansion of Europe in the last decades of the 15th century. Divided among loosely organized states, China was vulnerable and defenseless to the superior military power of the West.

This negative evaluation of Admiral He's ocean voyages has been rightfully corrected by China's decision to celebrate, in 2005, the 600th anniversary of the voyages by holding international conferences and mounting a very informative exhibition that made the rounds of different countries including the Philippines. The last part of the conference discussed the long-lasting outcome of the voyages. On balance, most of the outcome is beneficial. The expeditions extended and consolidated the maritime silk route, at the time when the land route was troubled, by expanding Mongol forces. They increased trade, commerce and deepened inter-cultural relations between China and Southeast Asia, as well as the rest of the world.

These three masters of Chinese ancient wisdom had one interest in mind: their goal was to transform the society. However, they use different methods and approaches. Confucius used the method of self-transformation; Zheng used the method of collaboration, and Sun Tzu in The Art of War sought to transform, not annihilate, the enemy through strategizing. These wisdom masters lived long before the current epoch. However, they have significant lessons for the business world today. They give us practical lessons in politics, business leadership, teamwork and management. The common interests, which were presented in Zheng He, Sun Zi, and Confucius' teachings, were providing alternative management and leadership models through adjustments to leadership style and thinking. While it is apparent that each of these leaders uses an approach which was different from others, it is clear that they had one major interest, objective and goal – gaining competitive advantage over your competitors. Indeed, much of human life and commercial activity is about having an upper hand over competitors, enemies, situations, difficulties, challenges and so on. Only those who afford to have an upper hand come out successfully. However, this has often been misunderstood.

For Admiral Zheng He, having an upper hand and a competitive advantage does not entail stepping on an enemy or competitor. Rather, it entails collaboration which is more of learning about the needs of others, reconciling interests, and forming relationships. From this point of view, at least, rivalry is diminished and there is no better environment for success than where rivalry has been eliminated. Rivalry is expensive. Where it is eliminated, we are able to focus on other goals necessary for self-improvement and self-advancement than self-defense.

Much of the world today is focusing on building alliances to improve both internal and external ties for military alliances and political and economic collaboration. This should never be misunderstood – their interest is the advantage they get from these different engagements which may range from sources of raw materials to market for their products. At the moment, China is using a very pragmatic approach in her relations with Africa while the West is using a measured approach just to be sure that they inculcate their culture and minimize risks. Indeed, cultural hegemony has always been of great importance to the West and it has tried to stamp it on the rest of the world through colonialism, language, and today we are talking about technology.

Having gone past the psycho-spiritual transformation evident in overcoming his religion, Zheng He was in a better position to address other problems and challenges facing countries. Collaborative leadership is the identification, release and union of the gifts for a certain purpose. We should here note that collaborative leadership is not for the common good but entails enriching the leader with different individual gifts through cooperation and participation so that his/her dream for leadership may be realized. Thus, collaboration is not possible if individuals concerned have not internalized some essential attitudes such as proactivity, personal leadership and management, interpersonal relationships and empathetic communication. This has great significance for Zheng He and for China. For Zheng He, it is for mutual economic and cultural benefits. For China, these have opened her to the rest of the world in spite of isolation by the West for being communist. These have resulted in her rapid progress.

The art of collaboration suits many of today's complex business situations better than the art of war. He believes that business networks and relationships are much more complex and intricate than in the past. This means that the battle lines are not always clear. Indeed, we have just come from the compartmentalization of the world ranging from the two great divides signified by the Berlin wall and the fall of the Soviet Union, between socialism cum communism and capitalism; we also have the Marxist divides between the haves (bourgeoisie) and those that have not (proletariats); we also have the divide between the North and the South.

Any sensible person will note that the world is naturally shifting from its past to its future. Market forces of demand and supply will tell you that the South has more power today and, therefore, the need for China to collaborate with Brazil, Japan, India and the whole of Africa and the rest of Asia. Probably the West has played a major role in strengthening the South especially Africa but critics and economists often bluntly argue that like Richard D.N. Dickson (1983) and Walter Rodney (1989) will tell you that much of the West's wealth has its cradle in Africa. Is China trying to follow suit? Is she a late comer? China has to stamp the authority of her numbers against all odds.

Whatever the case, China has to use a different approach from the one used by the West – her leadership has to shift from domination to collaboration. Seah Choo Meng puts this rightly in Professor Hum Si Hoon's book (2012): Rivalry is inherent in our fiercely competitive business world. While competition would undoubtedly provide the necessary impetus for a company to improve its business acumen and viability, mutual respect and peaceful coexistence are the very essence of your continued survival. Collaboration therefore plays an important role in enhancing a company's relationship with its competitors, one that would create mutually beneficial and much vaunted 'win-win' relationships.

Likewise, Welch's actions were very much driven by his belief that leaders should manage less and lead more, urging his people to focus less on micro-managing every single aspect of their departments, and focusing more on the bigger picture. By placing trust in his subordinates and encouraging them to do the same, Welch was able to drive through innovative, transformational policies that may otherwise have fallen by the wayside had his attention been focused on the minutiae which has clogged up many corporate leader's minds.

At a certain point, collaborative leadership needs to turn into strategic leadership and management, something which both Welch and Sun Tzu, were incredibly adept at doing. This is Sun Zi's idea. Strategizing, of course, entails meticulous and lengthy preparations, unity so as to advance together, swiftness, and time consciousness. However, one has to be aware of their resources to make sure that they do not exhaust them before engaging on the ultimate engagement. This is a common mistake made by business people and as such, they start their business already preoccupied and fatigues.

Business has often been thought of as a game without ethics. Indeed, most managers have a tendency to shelve human values at the expense of productivity and profit. Theorists and philosophers have argued for utilitarianism and the principle of teleology, pragmatism and so forth. For Confucius, business is something else and must pursue self-improvement as demonstrated and exercised in relating properly with others (Relating properly with others will entail using all the Sun Zi's Art of War tactics.)

THE METHODS

Zheng He, Sun Zi and Jack Welch would all have agreed that meticulous planning and attention to detail were key factors for success. All three were firmly focused on their ultimate goal; however, their planning styles were different – Zheng He approached planning with love and mercy toward all; whereas Sun Zi approached planning with careful regard paid toward learning the ways of the enemy, as one could overcome them easier, and Jack Welch had a very inclusive attitude, bringing his subordinates into the fold, and empowering them to be part of the process: encouraging everyone to embrace the inevitable changes and challenges which lay ahead, leaving him free to expand his corporate horizons.

THE METHODS FOR TRANSFORMATIONAL LEADERSHIP AND MANAGEMENT PLANNING

Getting out of the present, prevalent, competitive, and combative lose-win mindset will take a lot of planning and strategizing. Management gurus have already put planning as one of the functions of management which recently got a boost from a new discovery called "strategic planning and management." This is about establishing a vision and mission which are to be guided not only by the objectives of the organization, but by the values for which the organization stands for.

TRUTH OR MISDIRECTION

Sun Zi was a strong advocate in the art of misdirecting opponents. He would misinform the enemy, by supplying false information to spies, this threw his enemy off so that he and his army could attack. He was a master of the feint, sending troops to an area he had no intention of attacking in order to draw enemy forces away from his true objective.

It is difficult to know whether Sun Zi would be honest with his troops, particularly with his immediate subordinates. His concern for morale would suggest he might mislead his own soldiers, provided it gave them a victory that would overcome later mistrust. One might suspect that it would be a disadvantage to be caught out in a lie such as "We won't skirmish today" if the path were actually leading to a known enemy encampment. Besides, an ill-prepared soldier is likely to die without inflicting casualties on the foe. On the other hand, the rank and file might be better kept in the dark about long-term objectives, to prevent an information leak due to desertion or capture.

By contrast, Admiral Zheng He, appeared honest and above board in his diplomatic dealings. He was generally dealing from a position of power, backed by his armada and wealth of trade goods. Since the long-term goal was to strengthen ties with allies, rather than to conquer enemies or to make treaties with neutral powers during conflicts, it was an advantage to follow a pattern of openness and reliability.

Sun Zi lived and fought in sixth-century China, prior to its unification from competing nation-states. Sun Zi is believed to have been a contemporary of Confucius, and some recommend studying his book from a Taoist point of view. But while admired and used by politicians and business mogul, The Art of War was written for military purposes. It emphasized defeating an enemy. Knowledge and force were vital in gaining victory.

Modern business is sometimes regarded as cut-throat competition, and the win-lose paradigm is often invoked. There may be greater wisdom, however, in seeking win-win encounters. Game theory shows that, in many cases, long-term cooperation can yield better results than ruthless competition.

The "Prisoners' Dilemma" is well known. If one prisoner betrays the other, the result is better for the betrayer and worse for the other. If both prisoners stay loyal to each other, they receive a minor punishment. However, if each betrays the other, the result is very poor for both. The best long-term strategy, if the two players will "play the game" several times, is to remain loyal. Only in a one-time situation might one person benefit by betraying the other.

In terms of business, one is unlikely to take over a rival company through only one marketing campaign, so it makes sense to plan for the long term. It is even less wise to bankrupt a supplier or customer by entering into a lopsided contract. Therefore, Zheng He's cooperative approach is more suited to business in the modern-day globalized era than Sun Zi's competitive style.

Furthermore, with the Internet and the specter that WikiLeaks or similarly minded individuals might expose corporate, as well as, diplomatic secrets, business organizations should emphasize sharing information, in a way, that leads to mutual advantage.

Welch also espoused openness and transparency; he advocated an inclusive culture with everyone from grassroots level, right the way up to corporate management, pulling their weight for the "team." While a certain level of deception, particularly when it comes to competitors is usually to be expected within corporate circles, and Welch, was undeniably ruthless in many of his business dealings, on the surface at least, his ideals seem to have stood the test of time.

From a social philosophy, Confucianism, thus, became a political philosophy: benevolence and kindheartedness were to be the right way of government. Only this behavior would contribute to a peaceful society in a state, and in turn to a strong nation that would be able to fend off all foreign challenges.

14. ZHENG HE'S MODERN SUCCESS & CASE STUDY

To find a modern day example of a country proactively seeking a path of prosperity by following the lead of Admiral Zheng He, then we need look no further than Singapore.

Situated at the end of the Malay Peninsula, Singapore was referred to in an ancient account, back in the third century as Pu Luo Chung. Historically it has been long viewed as a desirable location and occasional safe haven by regional neighbors, with the Mongol Empire sending a trade delegation to Long Ya Men in 1320 and found itself in the middle of a military tug of war between Siam and the Majapahit Empire in the fourteenth century as they fought a contentious battle over the Malaysian Peninsular.

The Portugese were the first European colonial power to seize control of Singapore, when they arrived at Malacca in 1509. This marked the beginning of a power struggle between European nations which would last for over three hundred years. It wasn't, however, until after Britain finally announced its intention to withdraw troops from the island in 1971 that Singapore following the template set out by Admiral Zheng He, of free trade and transparency began its metamorphosis into the economic powerhouse that it is today. And although Singapore benefits from the free market economy, the government follows Zheng He's principle of ensuring that the general population benefits from private enterprise.

CHANGI AIRPORT

Following extensive consultations, the government of Singapore took a decision in 1975 to build a new flagship airport that would replace Singapore International Airport. Construction of the new airport, which would become known as Singapore Changi Airport, was one of the largest development products ever to be undertaken in the country's entire history. Today, the airport is owned by the Changi Airport Group and housing a whole plethora of airlines, including Singapore Airlines, Silk Air and Tigerair. The Changi Airport has won many global awards and accolades.

The airport's expansion policy is just one example of how the owners have adopted Zheng He's philosophies; constantly looking to the future, and thinking ahead and staying ahead of demand by successfully working with the constraints that it has in terms of space and factoring this into its building plans. Therefore, this airport has successfully avoided the congestion problems, frequently experienced by passengers at the likes of London's Heathrow Airport. Consequently, Changi Airport is in a prime position to meet all current and future passenger needs.

HOUSING DEVELOPMENT BOARD (HDB)

Owned by the government, HDB provides affordable, quality homes to its citizens. By always planning ahead and applying Zheng He's philosophies, of decency, integrity and fairness, the HDB also provides entire towns and communities with a whole range of social, commercial and recreational facilities. They are currently embarking upon an ambitious 20-30 year plan to transform existing properties and estates into world leading state of the art for homes.

The government of Singapore, with its policy and exemplary record of supporting big businesses which benefit the people, is the epitome of Zheng He's ideologies. I have cited just two examples in Changi Airport and HDB, when in reality I could easily have cited many, many, more such as the education, administrative and legal systems, Jurong islands' development and other government-owned companies such as Singapore Airline, Keppel Corporation etc.. By successfully balancing profit, with the welfare of its citizens it is a beacon of light in what can sometimes feel like a very dark world. Perhaps, if other nations to follow Singapore's example by adopting similar policies, then the world would be a more balanced and harmonious place in which to live. Let us study another successful case study of the use of Zheng He's lessons in modern day corporation in China.

CASE STUDY: THE ALIBABA GROUP

I have already discussed, how by adopting the principles and transformational philosophies as espoused by Admiral Zheng He, global conglomerates, large organizations and even countries can prosper. In the previous chapter, I talked about Singapore, and I have also examined the success of well- known brands, such as Apple. I would now like to focus specifically on the Alibaba Group: a Chinese company that by meticulously following the path charted by Zheng He, has risen from its formation in the humble apartment of current CEO Jack Ma, to become one of the largest groups of internet based companies in the world: who in 2012 outsold both Amazon and Ebay combined, with a staggering $170 billion in sales.

At the time of writing the Alibaba Group is currently comprised individual companies: Alibaba.com, China Vision Media Group, China Yahoo, Taobao, Tmall.com, Alipay, eTao, AliExpress, Alibaba Cloud Computing and Laiwang. Judging by the company's previous track record, then this number could easily increase over the coming years, and the scope of this book is not big enough to offer up a detailed analysis of each and every one. However, with the Alibaba Group now heading towards a stock market launch (IPO), then I would like, however, to focus on a couple, which I feel, best showcase Zheng He's ideals. Namely those of transparency and openness; the very cornerstone on which the internet was first founded!

ALIBABA.COM

If Admiral Zheng He were alive today, then he would be running a company exactly like Alibaba.com. As someone who believed in free trade, then he would have grasped with both hands the opportunities to be reaped from being the world's largest online business to business trading platform for small businesses.

Staying true to its core values of helping small businesses grow, while making profits for itself, Alibaba.com not only gives fledgling companies the opportunity to network and trade with each other, but it also runs a transaction based retail website, AliExpress.com, enabling those buyers with smaller needs to purchase lesser amounts at wholesale prices.

ALIPAY

With around 300 million users and control of around half of China's online payment market, Alipay which was founded in 2004 is an online payment platform with no transaction fees.

Staying true to Zheng He's principles of integrity and fairness, and concerned by what it calls China's weak consumer protection laws, it offers an escrow service to customers, enabling them to check that they are happy with the quality of their goods, before releasing payment to the retailer.

The company was restructured in 2010 following licensing regulations imposed by China's Central bank, and is now listed as a domestic company, run by its CEO Jack Ma; a modern day Zheng He.

15. CONCLUSION: ANCIENT SOLUTIONS TO CURRENT PROBLEMS

Throughout the course of this book, I have discussed how ancient Chinese wisdom continues to influence modern Chinese practices through the present day and how all businesses would benefit from using the corporate transformation techniques. In particular, I have looked at how by using the three phase surgical approach and incorporating the philosophies of Zheng He, Sun Zi and Confucius, shrewd businessmen, such as Jack Welch of G.E have transformed ailing businesses into global giants. I have also shown how enlightened politicians and business executives been able to seize the competitive edge and directly challenge the once seemingly indomitable United States of America, to make China the emerging economic powerhouse that it is today.

Following the example set by Sun Zi, Jack Welch was absolutely ruthless in downsizing G.E. He realized that in order for a corporate business to survive, then you had to be, if not the number one player in your chosen market then certainly number two as failure to maintain this advantageous position would inevitably result in your business being restructured, downsized or sold off by asset strippers. Sun Zi, with his brutal use of military tactics and ruthless, clinical approach to carrying out campaigns, best epitomizes the Surgical approach, However, Zheng He also demonstrated a hardline attitude in his cynical ad well thought out routing out of the pirates, and Confucius advocated stringent codes of conduct.

When it came to the second stage (resuscitation) Jack Welch, by putting in place a growth plan through the acquisition of carefully targeted businesses, adopted an approach consistent with the one first implemented by Zheng He, who through his numerous voyages to key trading partners, launched a charm offensive and built a huge network of people receptive to his advances as well as an enormous amount of goodwill, which translated into far more sales than he would otherwise have achieved.   Confucius's strong emphasis on family loyalty and the notion that the family is king is an endearing one, and has proved to be the cornerstone on which many successful Chinese businesses have been formed.

At some point during the third phase of corporate transformation (therapy) Jack Welch by establishing Crotonville and investing a lot of his own time an energy in the training of his younger managers, and promoting the power of teamwork and positivity, earned himself the title of "transformational Jack" Perhaps he looked to Sun Zi, who fully understood the need to boost his soldier's morale, or possibly Zheng He, who was a strong proponent of this phase: by choosing to travel with his troops, instead of staying in the comfort and security of his palace he was able to gather together over three thousand people, to travel with him on his long and incredibly dangerous voyages.

While the three phase approach is crucial to any corporate leader seeking to undergo transformation, the ancient Chinese philosophers also had other qualities which set them apart from the pack. For example, Confucius realized that in order to fully empower and embolden their staff, then they needed to be collaborative, visionary and constantly striving for win-win situations. A forward thinking, progressive and compassionate leader must learn to act decisively, with firmness and also diplomacy. They must do what is right, not just for himself but crucially, what is right for the company and its stakeholders. As such, transformational leadership brings together strategic thinking on team building behind Art of War; the golden rule proposed by Confucius; and the compassion, moderation and humility espoused by Lao Tzu.

Confucius had an extraordinary and noble vision for the world as he saw it, and while certain elements of Confucianism are not without their flaws, and are not wholly fit for purpose in a modern, increasingly egotistical world, there is still an awful lot that business leaders can derive from his teachings. Any discussion on Confucius would not be complete without mentioning the I Ching; the timeless guidebook seized upon by those seeking clarity and enlightenment in their lives, initially written by Fu Xi and expanded upon and enriched by Confucius. The I Ching, is possibly the singular most tangible and easily accessible reminder of Confucius, that is available to us today.

We have already discussed how Sun Zi, was the ultimate

strategist and how his brutal analysis of how war should be conducted is key to anyone planning on undertaking the first (Surgical) phase of the three stage plan. 'The Art of War' has been studied in depth not just by military strategists, and politicians but increasingly by business leaders the world over. With large swathes of the world's population embroiled either in acts of war against others, or facing major economic crises; or both, then The Art of War is as relevant today as it was when it was first written, and few could dispute the fact that the book offers an abundance of sage advice.

As Jack Welch demonstrated, any company facing the challenges of shrinking markets and lost profits must re-invent itself and fast. Corporate transformation, guided by a blend of sound Western business practices and ancient Chinese wisdom has proved itself as being effective time, and time again. Businesses unfortunate, or lucky enough, depending upon your perspective to find themselves in dire financial straits, must choose whether they are going to grasp around for short term solutions and risk being stripped down, or sold off, or whether they are going to follow the path of the great transformational leaders.

While Sun Zi, and Confucius have had a major influence on the way corporate entities conduct their business, it is possibly Zheng He that the world as a whole, needs to turn to as the torch-bearer to show us the way ahead. In the age of the internet and ever increasing accessibility, businesses of all shapes and sizes now have access to global markets in a way that would have been unthinkable even twenty years ago. Goodwill generates goodwill. Transparency is critical and diplomacy solves more problems than wars. The world is upside down at the moment, as faced with the consequence of the Republican Party starting wars in Iraq and Afghanistan, the Democratic Obama administration has looked incredibly weak and ineffective in its handling of the crises in Syria and Ukraine, and with the emergence of ISIS in Iraq, who knows how this is all going to end? Likewise, China would be wise to look to Zheng He as an example of how to conduct its international affairs, as its recent aggression in the South China Sea, has unnecessarily raised tensions in the area.

I have talked about corporate and political leaders, however we can all as individuals benefit from personal transformation. Not only do we need to revive our filial respect, but we need to extend it and reach out compassionately in all directions. We must then strive to understand the measures that need to be taken in order to bring about transformation and revitalization in the socioeconomic areas. Personal and economic growth only happens where the will exists to enable the seeds to grow, and for it thrive. If we really think that we can overcome the challenges, discord and distrust that has existed between nations since time began, then, collaboration is vital, and we need to set aside our reservations and co-operate with each other in the spirit in which the ancients intended.

We need to always plan ahead and strategize. We cannot continue living blindly as if we have no sense of direction. Strategizing means making plans for improvement and for change. Change is inevitable, but we must never allow it to ambush us like a tornado, and so we must learn to anticipate and manage it. For example, an unplanned or unexpected pregnancy can cause a major dilemma within a family unit. It is one of many problems that we would be best doing our utmost to avoid. The solution therefore is to plan for and anticipate change. Indeed, living fully is changing fully. We cannot be satisfied by being stagnant. We cannot just sit there; we need to do something. We further have to think about realistic change – not virtual change, not change which is merely a mirage. According to L. David Brown (1983), change means interventions to reframe perspectives.

Interventions to reframe perspectives includes reformulating party interests, altering unrealistic stereotypes, changing perspectives on the situation, and educating parties about the dynamics of conflict. Interventions to reframe perspectives depend on how new information is used and interpreted, if they are to change participants' interests, stereotypes, and understanding of the situation and its dynamics… Changing perspectives is a particularly powerful intervention when unrealistic stereotypes have strong emotional overtones, such as stereotypes associated with symbolic issues at culture interfaces, or stereotypes of upper and lower parties at level interfaces. Reframing perspectives can influence the interaction among representatives or the interplay of parties, context, and interface…But interventions that reframe perspectives can be undermined by cycles of behavior and communication that are inconsistent with new perceptions. New perceptions that are not complemented by changed behavior and communication do not last. Changed perspectives can also be undercut by unchanging pressures from parties and the larger context.

On a special note, these three philosophers, namely, Zheng He, Sun Zi and Confucius present to us a platform for understanding transformational leadership and management today. It is a process which entails a variety of elements and approaches. It's simply moving from the tradition – changing strategies, tactics and approaches – since goals have already changed. To be successful, you have to move with the demands and always adapt and adopt the changes that have taken place without delay. The faster you do this, the earlier you adapt.

The significance of ancient Chinese wisdom may not be known unless it is subjected to a modern day critique, similar to the one that I have carried out in this book. In any case, it may only remain a religious dogma or a cultural practice which has no effect on what happens outside culture and religion. A good critique of ancient Chinese wisdom simply tells us of what is to be, basically, obtained for us to reach the much craved for world peace, economic stability, socio-cultural interaction without any discrimination, sustainability, resolution of environmental challenges such as deforestation and pollution, love and so on. They simply tell us ethics are more important than profit; community is more important than an individual; and proper practical strategies are more valuable than wealth and long training and preparations which basically entail mere theory.

The first thing to note is that there was a time that China was the superpower. How and why? What elements led to her downfall? Chinese philosophy (Confucianism) is always taken to be the cause but in the real sense, ideological competition and improper appropriation of Sun Tzu's Art of War led to more wars and since China was peacefully lying in her bed contemplating, she never realized until she was told. China has now woken up drawing from her ancient wisdom sources and having them applied elsewhere.

Looked at with modern eyes, it is necessary for a shift from the tradition of competition, combat, conflict, confrontation, aggression to a totally new level of collaboration, cooperation, participation, communication, diplomacy and so forth. These have, of late, been found to be important and very effective in regional and international relations and trade which no longer aim at humiliating each other but creating a win-win situation. Obama's negotiation with countries like Lebanon, Syria, and Iran can be seen from this perspective. However, the recurring stalemate between Russia and Western allies (Great Britain, United States and France) are evident of the fact that the tradition of humiliation and win-lose competition is not totally gone. In a way, this reflects more the ideological differences between socialism cum communism against capitalism cum "democracy".

Today's political and business environment presents to us

different options which may need to be dealt with according to the context. However, no approach should be taken to be better than the others. In any case, one should always try to reconcile the three since, though they might have different values, their values are important in every case. Collaboration is more important for internal consolidation and for attracting and embracing external resources. This is more important especially in the marketing environment today. Collaboration will first entail harnessing the strengths and aptitudes of collaborators, building teamwork, reducing resistance, and ultimately having a wider market for ones products. Organizations have to learn to strike deals and to build concerted efforts with other organizations to give them better bargaining power and a kind of uniform and harmonious approach to that which affects them in common. Similarly, business knowledge today has to be guided by the knowledge that the business environment today is like a battlefield. It is apparent that competition, conflict of interest will never miss in business. But these can be approached without aggression and/or confrontation. As such, some tactics have to be used. To place Sun Zi's philosophies in a modern day setting, then a business that fails to plan and strategize plans and strategizes for failure. By adopting the ancient Chinese Wisdom as espoused by Sun Zi, Zheng He and Confucius and incorporating that said wisdom into your day to day business affairs, then I hope that I have demonstrated that you will have a business that is not only fit for purpose, but one that is able to utilize all that modern technology has to offer; trade freely in market places, both existing and new, including the plethora of virtual marketplaces which have sprung up courtesy of the world wide web and above all prosper and expand into a profitable and successful enterprise.

REFERENCES

1. Date: May 2011, Source:US Treasury Department, Website:http://www.treasury.gov/resource-center/data-chart-center/tic/Documents/mfh.txt

2. Date: September 01st 2011, Source: "Global Forecast Update" – Bank of Nova Scotia, Website: http://www.scotiacapital.com/English/bns_econ/fo recast.pdf

3. Source: Woodrow Wilson, War Messages, Location: 65th Cong., 1st Sess. Senate Doc. No. 5, Serial No. 7264, Washington, D.C.,1917; pp. 3-8, passim

4. Date of Publication: 01st October 2005, Date Retrieved: 15th February 2010, Source: Schoenherr Steven, "Undeclared Naval War in the Atlantic 1941." Location: History Department at the University of San Diego.

5. Source(s): Choe, Yong-ho., Lee, Peter H., and de Barry, Wm. Theodore., eds. Sources of Korean Tradition, Chichester, NY, Publisher: Columbia University Press, p. 419, 2000.

6. Source: Griffith, page 50: ISBN 0-19-501476-6.

7. Source: "I Ching (The Meanings of the 8 Trigrams and 64 Hexagrams)" Website: http://www.paranormality.com/i_ching_hexagram _meanings.shtml

8. Source: "100 Fastest-Growing Companies" for 2010,Website:http://money.cnn.com/magazines/for tune/fortunefastestgrowing/2010/full_list/.

9. Source: "Zhongpin: Overstated Income, Excessive Capex and Deceptive SAIC Filings" Website:

http://seekingalpha.com/article/287972-zhongpin-overstated-income-excessive-capex-and-deceptive-saic-filings

10. Website: http://en.wikipedia.org/wiki/Zheng_He

11. Website:http://www.sinodefenceforum.com/military-history/zheng-he-1371-1433-chinese-muslim-admiral-1449.html

12. Website:http://asianhistory.about.com/od/china/p/zheng_he_bio.htm

13. Website:http://english.chinamil.com.cn/site2/special-reports/2005-07/13/content_249001.htm

14. Website:http://pages.uoregon.edu/inaasim/Hist%20487/Spring%202006/Biography%20of%20Admiral%20Zheng%20He.htm

15. Website:http://asianhistory.about.com/od/glossaryae/g/GlosEunuch.htm

16. Source(s): Hoon, Hum Sin and Chew Lusheng Grace. "The Art of Collaboration: A Management

17. Date: June 2010, Publisher: NUS Business School, Source: Perspective Drawn From the Grand Voyages of Admiral Zheng He." Source: Sen, Tan Ta. "Cheng Ho, and Cultural Exchange in the Context of Southeast Asia."

18. Date: 2002, Publisher: Prentice Hall, Source: Teng, Michael. "Corporate Turnaround: Nursing A Sick Company Back to Health,"

19. Date: 2008, Publisher: Corporate Turnaround Centre Pte Ltd., Source:

20. Teng, Michael. "Training Manual: Corporate Turnaround and Transformation"

21. Date 2010, Publisher: Corporate Turnaround Centre Pte Ltd, Source: Teng, Michael. "Toolkit:

Corporate Transformation to improve productivity
and innovation"

ABOUT THE AUTHOR

Dr. Teng has a Doctor of Business Administration (D.BA) degree from the University of South Australia a Master's of Business Administration (M.BA), and a Bachelor of Mechanical Engineering (B.ENG) from the National University of Singapore. He is also a Professional Engineer (P Eng, Singapore), Chartered Engineer (C Eng, UK), and Fellow Member of several prestigious professional institutes, such as, Chartered Institute of Marketing (FCIM), Chartered Management Institute (FCMI), Institute of Mechanical Engineers (FIMechE), Marketing Institute of Singapore (FMIS), and Institute of Electrical Engineers (FIEE); he is a Senior Member of the Singapore Computer Society (SMSCS). He is also a Practicing Management Consultant (PMC) certified by the Singapore government.

Dr. Teng is widely recognized by the news media as a turnaround CEO in Asia. His subject of interest is corporate turnaround and transformation, as well as, internet marketing. He has been, on many different occasions, interviewed by the international media, such as, Malaysian Business Radio, BFM 89-9, News Radio FM 93.8, Malaysian Business Radio, Edge Radio (USA), the Channel News Asia, The Boss Magazine, Economic Bulletin, the Today, World Executive Digest, Lianhe ZaoPao, StarBiz, and the Straits Times. His online seminars are broadcast in over 120 countries via Success University and Skyquest.Com.

Dr. Mike Teng is the author of a best-selling book Corporate Turnaround: Nursing a Sick Company Back to Health, which was published in 2002. The book was translated into Bahasa, Indonesia, and Mandarin and was endorsed by both management guru Professor Philip Kotler and business tycoons Mr. Oei Hong Leong and Dr. YY Wong. Dr. Teng has subsequently authored more than twenty five management books.

Dr. Teng is appointed by the Singapore government as the national trainer to coach and instruct displaced senior managers and deploy them to run SMEs. He has more than 29 years of experience in corporate turnaround and transformation as well as engaged in strategic planning and handling operational management responsibilities in the Asia Pacific region. In these areas of expertise, he has held positions such as Chief Executive Officer for 20 years in multi-national and publicly listed companies. He was the CEO of a U.S. MNC based in Singapore for ten years. He spearheaded the turnaround of several troubled companies. He also advised several boards of directors of publicly listed companies.

Dr. Teng served as an Executive Council member for fourteen years and the last four years as the President of the Marketing Institute of Singapore (2000 – 2004), the National Marketing Association. He was the Chairman of the Chartered Management Institute (UK), Singapore branch and past President of the University of South Australia. He is currently the President of the National University of Singapore, M.BA Alumni.